The Nature of Salvation

The Nature of Salvation

JOHN WESLEY

BETHANY HOUSE PUBLISHERS
MINNEAPOLIS, MINNESOTA 55438
A Division of Bethany Fellowship, Inc.

Published by Bethany House Publishers
A Division of Bethany Fellowship, Inc.
6820 Auto Club Road, Minneapolis, Minnesota 55438

Printed in the United States of America

Library of Congress Cataloging-in-Publication Data

Wesley, John, 1703–1791.
˷˷˷The nature of salvation.

   (The Wesley library for today's reader)
   1. Salvation—Early works to 1800. I. Weakley, Clare G. II.
Title. III. Series: Wesley, John, 1703–1791. Wesley library for
today's reader.
BT750.W47   1987   234   87–21823
ISBN 0–87123–975–2

Dedication

This book is dedicated to
Murney and Max Call
in appreciation for their continual
Christian dedication, witness, and loving support.

JOHN WESLEY (1703–1791) was the founder of Methodism. Although raised in a godly home and trained for the ministry at Oxford, Wesley's failure as a missionary to the colonists and Indians in Georgia (1735–1738) revealed his unsaved condition. Strongly influenced upon his return to England by the Moravian, Peter Boehler, Wesley was converted (May 1738) to genuine faith in Christ while reading Luther's preface to Romans.

Shortly after his conversion, Wesley visited the Moravian settlement at Herrnhut and met Count Zinzendorf. He returned to England and embarked on his lifework. His objective was "to reform the nation, particularly the Church, and to spread Scriptural holiness over the land." He declared that he had only "one point of view—to promote, so far as I am able, vital, practical religion; and by the grace of God to beget, preserve, and increase the life of God in the souls of men." Some have viewed him as the eighteenth-century apostle commissioned to evangelize Great Britain.

Wesley discovered the most effective medium for reaching the masses was open-air preaching, and his life became one of an itinerant preacher. Facing the Church's resistance to his evangelical doctrine, Wesley formed societies in the wake of his mission. The organization of Methodism was thus a direct outcome of his success in preaching the gospel. Wesley's writings include his now classic *Journals*, sermons, letters, expositions, tracts, histories, and abridgments.

CLARE WEAKLEY, JR. is a businessman, lecturer, and chaplain-at-large in his community. He received a B.B.A. and an M.Th. from Southern Methodist University. He is married and he and his family make their home in Dallas.

Preface

To candid, reasonable men, I am not afraid to reveal what have been the inmost thoughts of my heart. I am a creature of a day, passing through life as an arrow in the air. I am a spirit come from God, and returning to God, just hovering over the great gulf—till, a few moments hence, I am no more seen; I drop into unchangeable eternity! I want to know one thing: the way to heaven—how to land safe on that happy shore. God himself has condescended to teach the way; for this very end He came from heaven. He has written it down in a book. Oh, give me that book! At any price give me the book of God! I have it—here is knowledge enough for me. Let me be a man of one book. Here, then, I am, far from the busy ways of men. I sit down alone; only God is here. In His presence I open and read His book that I may find the way to heaven. Is there a doubt about what I read? Does anything appear dark or intricate? I lift up my heart to the Father of Lights: "Lord, is it not Thy word, 'If any of you lack wisdom, let him ask of God'? Thou 'giveth to all men liberally, and upbraideth not.' Thou hast said, 'If any man will do his

7

will, he shall know.' I am willing to do. Let me know Thy will."

I then search after and consider parallel passages of scripture, "comparing spiritual things with spiritual." I meditate on them with all the attention with which my mind is capable. If any doubt remains, I consult those who are experienced in the things of God; and then the writings whereby, being dead, they yet speak. And what I thus learn, that I teach.

John Wesley
Sermons on Several Occasions
(London: The Epworth Press, 1944),
Preface, paragraph 5, page vi.

Table of Contents

Table of Contents

Introduction

Some sage left us an unforgettable theological truth when he said, "There are as many denominations as there are people." Certainly, every Protestant standing upon the right to interpret Scripture for himself will arrive at a personal theological opinion. Such personal opinions can deviate from those of John Wesley in many ways. Mine do. Wesley, however, is one of those theological giants who deserves to be heard. His theological and social impact on the Western world commands us to listen.

After twenty years of Wesleyan study, I find he has influenced my thinking in many ways, mostly for the better. I have read his *Journal* and sermons many times; I have spoken them into a tape recorder; I have edited, abridged, and published them. I therefore think I understand his message.

Wesley made me rise to a higher spiritual and intellectual level. He challenged both my ideas and my lifestyle as a self-professed Christian. While I fall far short of meeting the Christian pattern he describes, I cannot fault his description. It is scriptural and correct.

Likewise, Wesley's doctrine of salvation is scriptural

and correct. There is no debate about salvation by faith through unmerited grace. There is no debate that thousands of hearers of this message have received salvation while simply listening to the miraculous gospel story as Wesley and the early "Methodists" preached it.

A debate continues, however, on the nature of salvation. What, exactly, is salvation? How is it received? What effect does it have on the life of the believer? Can it be lost? If so, how? Why is it necessary? How did this come about in God's creation? What are God's plans for mankind, both saved and unsaved? And, why does all this matter to us anyway, considering the demands of daily living in the world?

John Wesley pondered these questions also. He left us abundant writings containing his answers. Read what he has to say about them. Let him challenge your thinking. Meditate and pray in the way he describes in the preface. If you will, you can receive a more exciting and fulfilling Christian life.

Clare George Weakley, Jr.

1

*God's Love to Fallen Man**

Not as the offense, so also is the free gift. (Romans 5:15)

How common, and how bitter, is the outcry against
Adam for the mischief which he not only brought upon
himself, but upon all his descendants. By his rebellion
against God, sin entered into the world. "By one man's
disobedience many were made sinners" (Rom. 5:19), deprived of God's favor, and His virtue, righteousness, and
true holiness. By Adam's sin we were sunk partly into the
image of the devil, susceptible to pride, malice, and all
other diabolical tempers. Likewise, death then entered
into the world, along with all its companions: pain, sickness, and a whole trail of uneasy, as well as unholy, passions and tempers.

For all this we may thank Adam. This charge has been
repeated in every age and every nation where the oracles
of God are known. Haven't you said the same thing? Most
who believe the biblical account of man's fall have had the
same thought concerning our first parent, and condemned

---

*From *Sermons on Several Occasions* (New York: Carlton and Porter,
1857 reprints), Sermon LXIV, Vol. 2, pp. 42–48.

him for his willful disobedience to the sole command of his Creator, bringing death and all our troubles into the world.

It would be well if the complaint stopped with Adam, but unfortunately it often glances off and hits God as well. Many, even those claiming to be Christians, have questioned God's mercy and justice on this point. Some have done this discreetly; but others have thrown aside care and asked, "Didn't God know Adam would abuse his liberty? Didn't He know the terrible consequences this would have on all mankind? Why did He permit Adam's disobedience when He could easily have prevented it?"

God certainly did foresee the consequences. No one denies that fact, for, "known unto God are all His works from the beginning of the world." God had power to prevent Adam's transgression, for He has all power in heaven and earth. At the same time, He knew it was best to allow it. He knew that permitting the fall of the first man was by far best for mankind in general. More good than evil would accrue to the followers of Adam by his fall. If sin abounded over all the earth, grace would much more abound, touching every individual of the human race except those choosing to reject grace.

It is strange that very little has been written, or at least published, on this subject. This idea has not been considered or understood by most Christians. It is not a matter of simple curiosity, but a truth of the deepest importance. How plain this important truth is to all thinking and candid inquirers. It is impossible, on any other principle, "to assert a gracious providence, and justify the ways of God with men."

May our loving Father open our eyes of understanding to perceive clearly that by Adam's fall all mankind has gained a new capacity to be more holy and happy on earth, and to be more happy in heaven, than otherwise they would have been.

⁓ The Benefits Gained by the Fall

By the fall of Adam, mankind in general gained a capacity of attaining more holiness and happiness on earth than would have been possible if Adam had not fallen. Without Adam's fall, Christ would not die. Nothing can be clearer than this, nothing more undeniable. The more thoroughly we consider the point, the deeper we shall be convinced of it. Unless all the partakers of human nature had received that deadly sin from Adam, it would not have been necessary for the Son of God to take our nature upon Him. This was the very reason for His coming into the world. "By one man sin entered into the world, and death by sin; and so death passed upon all." It was to remedy this very thing that the Word was made flesh, that as in Adam all died, so might all meet Christ and be made alive in Him.

If many had not been made sinners by the disobedience of one, many would not have been made righteous by the obedience of one. So there would have been no room for that amazing display of Jesus' love to mankind, and no occasion for His being obedient unto death, even the death of the cross. Never could it have been said, to the astonishment of all, "God so loved the world [the ungodly world, which had no thought or desire of returning to Him], that he gave his only begotten Son that whosoever believeth in him should not perish, but have everlasting life." Without Adam's fall, we could never say, "God was in Christ reconciling the world unto himself," or that He "made him to be sin [a sin offering] for us, who knew no sin, that we might be made the righteousness of God in him." There would have been no occasion for such an Advocate with the Father as Jesus Christ the Righteous or for His appearing at the right hand of God to make intercession for us.

Observe the obvious consequence of this. There would have been no such thing as faith in God thus loving the world, giving His only Son for us and for our salvation. There would have been no such thing as faith in the Son of God, who loves us and gives himself for us. There would have been no faith in the Spirit of God, who renews us in the image of God in our hearts and raises us from the death of sin into the life of righteousness. Indeed, the whole gift and privilege of justification by faith could not have existed. There could have been no redemption in the blood of Christ, nor could Christ have been "made unto us" either "wisdom, and righteousness, and sanctification" or "redemption."

The same great void which was in our faith, also would have been in our love. We might have loved the Author of our being, the Father of angels and men, as our Creator and Preserver. We might have said to Him, "Oh, Lord our Governor, how excellent is thy name in all the earth," but we could not have loved Him under the nearest and dearest relation, "as delivering up his Son for us all."

We might have loved Jesus as being "the brightness of his [Father's] glory, and the express image of his person," but we could not have loved Him as bearing "our sins in his own body on the tree," and "by that one oblation of himself once offered making a full sacrifice, oblation, and satisfaction for the sins of the whole world." We could not have been "made conformable unto his death" nor have known "the power of his resurrection."

We could not have loved the Holy Spirit for revealing to us the Father and the Son, for opening the eyes of our understanding, for bringing us out of the darkness into His marvelous light, and renewing the image of God in our soul and sealing us unto the day of redemption.

What is now "pure religion and undefiled," would then have had no being. All these events depend on those grand principles: "By grace are ye saved through faith" and Jesus Christ is of God "made unto us wisdom, and righteousness, and sanctification, and redemption."

We see, then, what advantage we derive from the fall of Adam, with regard to faith. It is a faith gained both in God the Father, who spared not His only Son but "wounded [Him] for our transgressions" and "bruised [Him] for our iniquities," and in God the Son, who poured out His soul for us transgressors and washed us in His own blood. Here is the advantage we receive with regard to the love of God, both of God the Father and God the Son. The first ground of this love, as long as we remain on earth, is clearly declared: "We love him because He first loved us." This greatest instance of His love could never have been known if Adam had not fallen.

As our faith, both in God the Father and the Son, receives its increase—if not its very being—from this event, also does our love both of the Father and the Son. So does the love of our neighbor, which increases in proportion to our faith and love of God. Everyone understands the lesson shown by the Apostle John, "Beloved, if God so loved us, we ought also to love one another." God so loved us—observe the stress of the argument lies on this very point, so loved us—as to deliver up His only Son to die for our salvation. What manner of love is this? God has so loved us, as to give His only Son, who in glory and in majesty is equal with the Father and coeternal! What sort of love is this? The only begotten Son of God has loved us and emptied himself, as far as possible, of His eternal Godliness. He divested himself of all the glory which He had with the Father before the world began, to take upon himself the form of a servant and be made as a man, then to humble himself still further, being obedient unto death, even the cruel death of the cross.

As God so loved us, we are to love one another. This

motive to brotherly love would have been totally lacking
if Adam had not fallen. Consequently, we could not have
loved one another in so high a degree as we may now.
Neither could there have been that height and depth in
Jesus' command, "That ye love one another, as I have loved
you." These gains we have by Adam's fall, regarding both
the love of God and of our neighbor.

There is another point which deserves our consideration. Through Adam not only sin but pain entered the
world and settled on mankind. But from this appears not
only the justice but the unspeakable goodness of God. How
much good He continually brings out of this evil; how
much holiness and happiness result from pain.

The benefits God conveys to us through sufferings are
innumerable. It could be said, "What are termed afflictions in the language of men, are in the language of God
styled blessings." Had there been no suffering in the
world, a considerable part of religion, and in some respects
the best part, may have never been known. Through suffering, our passive graces are built, including the noblest
of all Christian graces—love that endures all things. Here
is the ground for resignation to God, enabling us to say
from the heart, in the most trying hour, "It is the Lord,
let Him do what seemeth Him good."

Here is the foundation for confidence in God, both with
regard to what we feel and with regard to what we should
fear. What room could there be for trust in God if there
were no such thing as pain or danger? Who might not say
then, "The cup which my Father hath given me, shall I
not drink it?" It is by sufferings that our faith is tried,
and, therefore, made more acceptable to God. It is in the
day of trouble that we have occasion to say, "Though he
slay me, yet will I trust in him." And this is well pleasing
to God, that we should claim Him in the face of danger
and in defiance of sorrow, sickness, pain, or death.

Also, had there been neither natural nor moral evil in the world, we could never have known patience, meekness, gentleness, or long-suffering. It is clear they could not have existed because all these have evil as their cause. Therefore, if evil had never entered into the world, neither could these qualities have any place in it. Who could have returned good for evil, had there been no evil? How would it be possible to overcome evil with good?

You might say, "But all these graces might have been divinely put into the hearts of men." Undoubtedly they might. But, if they had, there would have been no need for them. In the present state of things, we always have occasions to use them. The more they are exercised, the more all our graces are strengthened and increased. And as they increase, along with our faith and love of God and man, our present happiness increases.

God's permission of Adam's fall also presented us with another advantage: the opportunity to do good in countless instances. This exercising of various good works otherwise could have had no being. What exertions of benevolence, of compassion, of godlike mercy, would then have been totally prevented? Who could then have said to the lover of men,

> Thy mind throughout my life be shown,
> While listening to the wretch's cry,
> The widow's or the orphan's groan,
> On mercy's wings I swiftly fly,
> The poor and needy to relieve,
> Myself, my all, for them to give?

A benevolent person knows, "All worldly joys are less, than that one joy of doing kindnesses." Surely in keeping this commandment, if no other, there is great reward. "As we have time, let us do good unto all men"—good of every kind and in every degree. Accordingly, the more good we do, the happier we shall be. The more we give our bread to the hungry and clothe the naked; the more we relieve the stranger and visit those who are sick or in prison; the more kind offices we do to those that groan under the various evils of human life, the more comfort we receive even in this world, and the greater joy we have in our own hearts.

The sum of this is: the more holy we are upon earth, the more happy we must be, because there is an inseparable connection between holiness and happiness. The more good we do to others, the more reward overflows into our own soul, even as our sufferings for God lead us to rejoice in Him "with joy unspeakable and full of glory." Therefore the fall of Adam, first by giving us an opportunity of being far more holy, then by giving us the occasions of doing innumerable good works, and, finally, by putting it into our power to suffer for God, is of such advantage to mankind even in the present life, that we cannot fully understand it before entering everlasting life.

Only in the presence of God shall we be enabled fully to comprehend both the advantages which accrue at the present time by the fall of Adam, and the infinitely greater advantages which we will reap from it in eternity. To form some conception of this, we should remember the observation, as "one star differeth from another star in glory, so also is the resurrection of the dead." The most glorious saints may be those who are the most holy, who bear most of the image of God in which they were created. Next in glory to these could be those who have done most good works. After them may come those who have suffered most, according to the will of God.

What advantages, in every one of these respects, will we receive in heaven, because God permitted pain on earth as a consequence of sin? Through pain we attained many holy qualities which otherwise could never have developed. On account of this superior holiness, we will then enjoy superior happiness. Everyone will then "receive his own reward, according to his own labor." Every individual will be "rewarded according to his work."

So the fall has given rise to innumerable good works which could otherwise never have existed, such as ministering to the saints and relieving distress of every kind, whereby innumerable saints will be added to the eternal crown. Again, there will be an abundant reward in heaven for suffering, as well as for doing the will of God. "Our light affliction, which is but for a moment, work out for us a far more exceeding and eternal weight of glory."

Therefore Adam's fall, which brought suffering into the world, has also brought an increase of glory to all eternity. All sufferings will be at an end there, yet the joys they produced shall never end, flowing from God's right hand forevermore.

There is one more large advantage that we reap from Adam's fall which is worthy of our attention. In Adam all died. If this were not the case, every descendant of Adam, every child of man, would have personally answered for himself to God. It is a necessary consequence of this that if one had once fallen, once violated any command of God, there would have been no possibility of his going to heaven. With no help, he must have perished without remedy. The word was: "The soul that sinneth, it shall die." Who would wish to hazard a whole eternity upon one act? It is much better to be in a state where, though burdened with weaknesses, we do not run such a desperate risk. If we fall, we may rise again through Christ.

Let me call every serious person to fix his attention on Christ. All that has been said, all that can be said, centers in this point: the fall of Adam produced the death of Christ. If God had prevented the fall of man, the Word would never have been made flesh. We never would have seen His glory, the glory as of the only begotten of the

Father. Those mysteries never would have been displayed. I think this consideration swallows up all the rest and should never be out of our thoughts. Unless by one man judgment had come upon all men to condemnation, no one could ever have known the unsearchable riches of Christ.

See then, upon the whole, how little reason we have to lament the fall of Adam, since from it we derive such unspeakable advantages—both in time and eternity. See how little reason there is for questioning the mercy of God in permitting that event to take place. Now, where is the one who presumes to blame God for not preventing Adam's sin? Should we not rather bless Him from the bottom of our hearts for laying the grand program for man's redemption and making way for the glorious manifestation of His wisdom, holiness, justice, and mercy?

If God had decreed, before the foundation of the world, that all people should dwell in everlasting burnings because Adam sinned before they existed, no one could thank Him for this except the devil and his angels. On that supposition, all those billions of unhappy spirits would be plunged into hell by Adam's sin without any possible advantage from it. But, blessed be God, this is not the case. Such a decree never existed. On the contrary, every one born may be a gainer from Adam's fall, and none ever was or can be a loser except by his own choosing.

We see here a full answer to an account of the origin of evil, which was published many years ago and supposed to be unanswerable, that "it necessarily resulted from the nature of matter, which God was not able to alter."

It is very kind of that sweet tongued orator to make an excuse for God, but there is really no need for it. God has answered for himself. He made man in His own image, a spirit endued with understanding and liberty. Man, abusing that liberty, produced evil and brought sin and pain into the world. God permitted this in order to show a fuller manifestation of His wisdom, justice, and mercy. By it, He bestowed on all who would receive it an infinitely greater happiness than could possibly have been attained if Adam had not fallen.

"Oh, the depth of the riches both of the wisdom and knowledge of God!" Although the particulars of His judgments and ways are unsearchable to us, and beyond our finding out, yet we may discern His general scheme running through time into eternity. "According to the counsel of His own will," the plan He had laid before the foundation of the world, He created the parent of all mankind, Adam, in His own image. Then He permitted all men to be made sinners by the disobedience of Adam so that by the obedience of one, all who receive the free gift of Christ's mercy may be infinitely holier and happier to all eternity!

2

*The Scriptural Way of Salvation**

Ye are saved through faith. (Ephesians 2:8)

Nothing can be more intricate, complex, and hard to understand than religion. This is not only true concerning heathen religion, but also concerning the religion of those who claim to be Christian. Yet how easily understandable, how plain and simple, is the genuine religion of Jesus Christ, provided only that we take it in its native form, just as it is described in the Bible. It is well-described by our wise God for the weak understanding and narrow mental capacity of man.

Observe this, both as to the end God proposes, as well as the means to attain that end. The end is, in one word, salvation, the means to attain it, faith.

It is easy to discern that these two little words, faith and salvation, are the essence of all that the Bible teaches. Being this important, we should take all possible care to avoid mistakes, and seek a true and accurate judgment

Op. cit., Sermon XLIII, Vol. 1, pp. 74–91.

concerning both of these concepts.

What Is Salvation?

Salvation is more than simply going to heaven with eternal happiness or ascending to that paradise Jesus called "Abraham's bosom." It is much more than the blessing which lies on the other side of death, in the other world. The very words of Paul's text put this beyond all question; "Ye *are* saved" is not something at a distance. It is present; a blessing which, through the free mercy of God, you may now possess. The words also may be rendered with equal propriety, "Ye *have been* saved." Thus, salvation is the entire work of God—from the first dawning of grace in the soul until it is completed in final glory.

Salvation includes all that is done in the soul by what is frequently termed natural conscience. More properly, this is *preventing* grace. It is all the drawings of the Father and the desires of God, which, when we yield to them, increase more and more by that light with which the Son of God graces everyone who comes into the world. He shows every man how to do justly, to love mercy and to walk humbly with his God. Included are all the convictions which His Spirit, from time to time, works in every person, although most men stifle them as soon as possible and later forget, or at least deny, they ever had them at all.

But now we are concerned only with that salvation of which Paul is directly speaking. This consists of two general parts, *justification* and *sanctification*.

Justification is simply another word for pardon. It is the forgiveness of all our sins, and our resulting acceptance by God. The price of this has been paid for us by the blood and righteousness of Jesus Christ—all that Christ has done and suffered for us, the pouring out of His soul for sinners. The immediate effects of justification are the peace of God—a peace that passes all understanding—and a rejoicing in the hope of the glory of God with unspeakable joy and full glory.

The moment we are justified, sanctification begins. In that instant we are born again, born from above, born of the Spirit. There is both a real as well as a relative change. We are inwardly renewed by the power of God. We have the love of God put directly into our hearts by the Holy Spirit who is given to us. His Spirit produces love to all mankind, and more especially to God's children. This event expels our love of the world, pleasure, ease, honor, and money. Also removed are pride, anger, self-will, and every other evil tempter. In a word, it is the miraculous changing of our earthly, sensual, devilish minds into the mind which was in Christ Jesus.

It is natural for those who experience such a change to imagine that all their sin is gone, utterly rooted out of their hearts, with none left. How easily does the reborn believe, "I feel no sin, therefore I have none! Sin does not stir, therefore it does not exist. It has no motion in me, therefore it has no being in me."

But it is seldom long before new Christians find sin was only suspended, not destroyed. Temptations return and sin revives, showing it was stunned but not dead. They now feel two principles in themselves, plainly contrary to each other. They experience the flesh lusting against the Spirit, nature opposing the grace of God. Although they still have power to believe in Jesus and to love God, and although His Spirit witnesses with their spirits that they are children of God, they find themselves sometimes in pride or self-will, sometimes in anger or unbelief. They find one or more of these sins frequently stirring in their heart, though not conquering. These are thrust at them, tempting them to fall, but the Spirit is their help in overcoming.

Macarius, hundreds of years ago, described this experience of God's children. "The unskillful, when grace operates, presently imagine they have no more sin. Whereas they that have discretion cannot deny that even we who have the grace of God may be molested again—for we have often had instances of some among the brethren who have experienced such grace as to affirm that they had no sin in them, and yet, after all, when they thought themselves entirely freed from it, the corruption that lurked within was stirred up anew, and they were well nigh burned up."

From the moment of our being born again, the gradual work of sanctification takes place. We are enabled by His Spirit to overcome the deeds of the body and our evil nature. As we are more and more dead to sin, we are more and more alive to God. We go on from grace to grace, being careful to abstain from all appearance of evil, being zealous of good works. As we have opportunity, we do good to all men. We walk blameless in all His requirements, worshiping Him in spirit and in truth, while we take up our cross and deny ourselves every pleasure that does not lead us to God.

Thus we wait for entire sanctification, with full salvation from all our sins, including pride, self-will, anger, and unbelief. As the Scripture expresses it, we go on to perfection. But what is perfection? The word has various senses but here it means perfect love. It is love excluding sin, filling the heart and taking up the whole capacity of the soul. It is love rejoicing always, praying without ceasing, and giving thanks in everything.

Saving Faith

Faith in general is defined by Paul as an evidence. It is divinely given evidence and conviction of things not seen, not visible, not perceivable by sight or by any of the external senses. It implies a supernatural evidence of God and of the things of God (a kind of spiritual light given to one's soul). Scripture speaks of God giving light and the ability to recognize it. Paul wrote, "God, who commanded the light to shine out of darkness, hath shined in our hearts, to give the light of the knowledge of the glory of God in the face of Jesus Christ." Elsewhere he speaks of "the eyes of [our] understanding being enlightened."

By this twofold operation of the Holy Spirit, having the eyes of our soul both opened and enlightened, we see the things which the natural eye has not seen and the physical ear has not heard. We experience the invisible things of God. We see the spiritual world, which is all around us, and no longer treat it as if it did not exist. We now see this eternal world piercing through the veil which hangs between time and eternity and discover the glory which shall one day be revealed in full.

Taking the word in a more personal sense, faith is a divine evidence and conviction, not only that God was in Christ reconciling the world to himself, but also that Christ loved me in particular, and gave himself for me. It is through this faith experience that we receive Jesus Christ. We receive Him in all His offices as our Prophet, Priest, and King. By this, God gives Him to us for wisdom, righteousness, sanctification, and redemption.

Is this the faith of assurance or the faith of adherence? Scripture makes no distinction between the two. Paul says there is "one faith," and "one hope of your calling." There is only one saving Christian faith, just as there is one Lord in whom we believe, and one God and Father of us all. Certainly this faith necessarily implies an assurance that Christ loved me and gave himself for me. Anyone who believes with the true living faith has the witness inside himself. "The Spirit witnesses with our spirit, that we are children of God."

"Because we are sons, God hath sent forth the Spirit of his Son into your hearts, crying, Abba, Father"; giving believers an assurance that they are children of the King, along with a childlike confidence in Him.

Let it also be observed, the assurance naturally comes before the confidence. One cannot have a childlike confidence in God until he knows he is a child of God. Therefore confidence, trust, reliance, adherence, or whatever else it is called, is not the first, but the second branch or act of faith.

How Faith Works

It is by this faith we are saved, justified, and sanctified. But how does faith accomplish this?

First, how are we justified by faith? Faith is the condition, and the only condition, of justification. Faith alone is sufficient for justification. Everyone who believes is justified, whatever else he has or lacks. In other words, no man is justified till he believes, and every man, when he believes, is justified.

But does not God command us to repent also? Yes, and also to bring forth the fruits of repentance. He requires us to cease, for instance, from doing evil, and to learn to do good. Both are necessary, for if we willingly neglect either, we cannot reasonably expect to be justified at all. But if this is so, how can it be said that faith is the only condition of justification?

Undoubtedly, God does command us both to repent and bring forth fruits of repentance. If we neglect this, we cannot reasonably expect to be justified at all. Therefore, both repentance and fruits of repentance are, in some sense, necessary to justification. However, these are not necessary in the same sense as faith, nor in the same degree.

Fruits of repentance are only necessary conditionally, as there is time and opportunity for them. It is possible for a person to be justified without them, as was the thief upon the cross. However, no one can be justified without faith. That is impossible. Likewise, one can repent and bring forth fruits of repentance, yet is not justified until he believes. But, the moment he believes, with or without the fruits and with any degree of repentance, he is justified. This is law in the same sense, for repentance and its fruits are only remotely necessary to faith, while faith is immediately and directly necessary to salvation. So it remains, faith is the only condition, immediately and proximately, necessary for salvation.

Exactly as we are justified by faith, so are we sanctified by faith. Faith, not works, is the condition, and the only condition, of sanctification, exactly as it is of justification. It is *the* condition. Only those who believe can be sanctified. Without faith, no man is sanctified. This alone is sufficient for sanctification. Everyone who believes is sanctified, whatever else he has or has not. In other words, no man is sanctified until he believes, and every man is sanctified when he believes.

It may be asked, is there a repentance after, as well as before, justification? And is it not required of all who are justified to be zealous to do good works? Are not these works so necessary that if one willingly neglects them, sanctification in the full sense cannot reasonably be expected?

Do not good works generate perfection in love, growth in all grace, and in the loving knowledge of our Lord Jesus Christ? Without repentance can one retain the grace which God has already given him and continue in the faith which he has received, remaining in the favor of God? If this is so, how can it be said that faith is the only condition of sanctification?

Of course there is a repentance after, as well as before, justification. Truly, all who are justified are required to be zealous of good works. These works are so necessary that if one *willingly* neglects them he cannot reasonably expect to ever be fully sanctified. Lacking these works, he cannot grow in grace in the image of God, obtaining the mind of Christ Jesus. Then he will not retain the grace he has received and continue in faith or in the favor of God.

The inference we must draw from this is that both repentance, *rightly understood*, and the practice of all good works—works of piety as well as works of mercy— are, in some sense, necessary to sanctification.

I say repentance rightly understood, for this must not be confused with the earlier repentance. Repentance after salvation is different from repentance which precedes it. After justification, repentance implies no guilt, no sense of condemnation, and no consciousness of God's wrath. It does not include any doubt of God's favor or any fear of punishment. It is a conviction, brought by the Holy Spirit, of the sin which still remains in our hearts, and of the carnal mind which remains, even in them who are saved. But that sin no longer reigns and no longer dominates us. We have victory over our tendency to evil, over a heart bent to backsliding, and over the still continuing tendency of the flesh to lust against the Spirit. Sometimes, unless we continually watch and pray, we lust to pride, sometimes to anger, sometimes to love of the world, love of ease, love of honor, or love of pleasure more than love of God. We are convinced of the tendency of our hearts to self-will, to idolatry, and above all to unbelief by which, in a thousand ways and under a thousand pretenses, we are ever departing—more or less—from our loving, living God.

Joined with this conviction of the sin remaining in our hearts is a clear conviction of the sin still remaining in our lives, cleaving to all our words and actions. In the best of our acts, we now discern a mixture of evil—either in the spirit, the matter, or the manner of them. There is always something that could not stand God's righteous judgment, were He exact in marking all our faults. Where we least expect it, we find a taint of pride or self-will, of unbelief or idolatry. The result is that we are now more ashamed of our best duties than we were formerly of our worst sins. Hence we can only feel that these are far from having anything meritorious in them. We are far from being able to stand in the sight of the divine justice. We know and feel that for those imperfections we are guilty before God except for the grace given by the blood of the covenant.

Experience, together with the conviction of sin remaining in our hearts, cleaving to all our words and actions, shows the guilt which we should incur were we not continually covered by Jesus' atoning blood.

One thing more is implied in this repentance: a conviction of our helplessness, of our utter inability to think one good thought or to form one good desire. We are unable to speak one word right or to perform one good action except through His free, almighty grace, first diverting us, and then accompanying us every moment.

Works and Sanctification

What good works are necessary to sanctification? First, all works of piety, such as public prayer, family prayer, private prayer, and receiving the supper of the Lord. Further, sanctification grows through searching the Scriptures, by hearing, reading, meditating, and using such fasting or abstinence as our bodily health allows.

Also, all works of mercy are included, whether they relate to the bodies or souls of men. This is feeding the hungry, clothing the poor, entertaining the stranger, visiting those who are in prison or sick or afflicted. Also, endeavoring to instruct the ignorant, to awaken the sinner, to quicken the lukewarm, to assure those wavering, to comfort the feebleminded, to comfort those in temptation, and contribute in every manner to the saving of souls. This is true repentance and the fruits for repentance which are necessary for full sanctification. This is the way God has directed us to follow for completion of our salvation.

Now consider the extreme danger of the seemingly innocent opinion that there is no sin in a believer and that all sin is destroyed—root and branch—the moment a man is justified. That claim blocks the way to sanctification by totally preventing repentance. There is no place for repentance in one who believes there is no sin either in his life or heart. Consequently there is no way for such a person to be perfected in divine love, to which repentance is absolutely necessary.

Hence it may appear that full sanctification is not possible. That may be the case, but the very expectation of full salvation, complete sanctification, encourages us to use all the talents God has given us. It calls us to improve our deeds so that when our Lord comes, He will receive His own works with increase through our works.

Faith Is the Key

So it is agreed that both this repentance and its fruits are necessary to full salvation, but they are not necessary either in the same sense as faith, or in the same degree. We say not in the same degree for these fruits are necessary conditionally, when there is time and opportunity for them, otherwise one may be sanctified without them. But no one can be sanctified without faith. Likewise, ever so much of this repentance or ever so many good works will not avail. One is not sanctified until he believes. At the moment one believes, with or without those fruits, and with more or less of this repentance, he is sanctified, though not in the same sense. This repentance and these fruits are only remotely necessary for the continuance of faith, as well as the increase of it. Faith is immediately and directly necessary to sanctification. It remains that faith is the only condition which is immediately and proximately necessary to sanctification.

God Does the Work

What is that faith whereby we are sanctified, saved from sin, and perfected in love? It is a divine evidence and conviction, first, that God has promised faith in the Bible. Until we thoroughly believe this, there is no moving ahead. Nothing more is needed to satisfy any reasonable person of this than the great promise, "The Lord thy God will circumcise thine heart and the heart of thy seed, to love the Lord thy God with all thine heart and with all thy soul." How clearly this expresses being perfected in love. This strongly implies being saved from all sin. As long as love takes up the whole heart, what space remains for sin?

Here is the divine evidence and conviction that what God has promised He is able to perform. Admittedly, with men it is impossible to bring a clean thing out of an unclean, to purify the heart from all sin, and to fill it with all holiness. However, this causes in us no difficulty because with God all things are possible. Surely no one ever imagined salvation and perfection were possible to any power less than that of the Almighty. If God speaks, it shall be done. God said, "Let there be light." Now there is light.

There is a divine evidence and conviction that He is able and willing to do it *now*. And why not? A moment to Him is the same as a thousand years. He does not need more time to accomplish whatever is His will. He cannot wait for any more worthiness or fitness in the persons He is pleased to save. Therefore we boldly say, at any time, "Now is the day of salvation!" "Today, if ye will hear his voice, harden not your hearts!" "All things are ready: come unto the marriage!"

To this confidence that God is both able and willing to save and sanctify us now, there needs to be added one more thing. We need divine evidence and conviction that He does it. Personal evidence comes the moment God says to your soul, "According to thy faith be it done unto thee!" Immediately the soul is pure from every spot of sin. It is clean from all unrighteousness. The believer personally experiences the deep meaning of those solemn words, "If we walk in the light as He is in the light we have fellowship one with another, and the blood of Jesus Christ, His Son, cleanseth us from all sin." The evidence is written on the believer's heart.

But does God work this sanctification in the soul gradually or instantaneously? Perhaps it may be gradually wrought in some. I mean in this sense, they do not know the particular moment when sin ceases to be. But it is most desirable, were it the will of God, that it should be done instantaneously.

The Lord can destroy sin by the breath of His mouth in a moment, in the twinkling of an eye. It is a plain fact that He generally does so, and there is evidence enough of this to satisfy most people. Therefore, look for it every moment. Look for it in the way I have described, in all those good works where you are created anew in Christ

Jesus. You can be no worse, if you become no better, because of your expectation. Even if you are disappointed in your hope, still you lose nothing. But you shall not be disappointed in your hope. It will come. Look for complete sanctification every day, every hour, every moment. Why not now, at this moment? Certainly you may look for it now, if you believe it is by faith. By this token you may surely know whether you seek it by faith or by works. If you seek salvation only by works, you want something to be done first, before you are sanctified. If you think, I must first be or do thus or thus, then you are still seeking it by works unto this day.

If you seek it by faith, you may expect it just as you are. If as you are, then expect it now. It is important to observe that there is an inseparable connection between these three points. Expect it by faith, expect it as you are, and expect it now. To deny one of them is to deny them all. To allow one is to allow them all.

Do you believe we are saved and sanctified by faith? Be true, then, to your principle. Look for this blessing just as you are, neither better nor worse, as a poor sinner that has still nothing to pay, nothing to plead, but Christ died and risen. And if you look for it as you are, then expect it now. Hold for nothing. Why should you? Christ is ready, and He is all you want. He is waiting for you. He is at the door. Let your inmost soul cry out, "Come in, come in, thou heavenly guest! Nor hence again remove, but sup with me and let the feast be everlasting love."

3

*The Lord Our Righteousness**

This is his name whereby he shall be called, The Lord our Righteousness. (Jeremiah 23:6)

The conflicts which have arisen about religion are dreadful and numberless. These occur among those who never knew true Christianity as well as among God's children—those who have experienced the kingdom of God within them along with righteousness, peace, and joy in the Holy Ghost. How many Christians, instead of joining together against their common enemy, Satan, have turned their weapons against one another. Thus they have wasted their precious time, hurt one another's spirits, weakened each other's works and hindered the great work of their Father. The result is many of the weak have been offended, many of the lame turned away from salvation, many sinners have been confirmed in their disregard of all religion and their contempt of those that profess it, and many of the faithful have been left in sorrow.

What would not every lover of God do, what would he

Op. cit., Sermon XX, Vol. 1, pp. 169–176.

not suffer to remedy this evil and remove contention from God's children—to restore or preserve peace among them? Nothing is too valuable to part with in order to promote this harmony. Suppose we cannot make religious wars cease. Suppose we cannot reconcile all the children of God to one another. Let us each do what we can to contribute toward it if it be but two minutes. Blessed are they who are able, in any degree, to promote peace and good will among men, especially among those under the banner of Jesus—who are required to live peaceably with all men, as much as they can.

It would be a considerable step toward this great end, if we could bring good men to understand one another. Disputes arise purely from the lack of understanding, from simple misapprehension. Contending parties often misunderstand what their opponent means. Then it follows that each violently attacks the other, even though there is no real difference between them. It is not always an easy matter to convince them of this, particularly when passions are high. Then it is most difficult. However, it is not impossible, especially when we trust in God, placing all our dependence upon Him with whom all things are possible. How quickly He disperses the cloud, shines into hearts and enables us to understand each other and His truth.

One great truth in the text is: "This is his name whereby he shall be called, The Lord our Righteousness!" This truth is deep in the nature of Christianity and supports the whole frame of it. Simply put, it says that Christ's righteousness, and not our own, is the source of our redemption—on this text the Christian church stands or falls. Certainly it is the pillar and ground of the faith which gives salvation. It is the foundation of the universal faith which is found in all God's children and which must be kept "whole and undefiled."

Therefore, one might expect all who claim Christ to agree on this point. But this is far from being the case. There is scarcely any text wherein there is so little agreement and where those who profess to follow Christ have so wide and irreconcilable differences. I say seem because I am totally convinced that many of them only seem to differ. Their disagreement is more in words than in sentiments. They are closer together in mind than in language. There certainly is a great difference in language, not only between Protestants and Catholics but also between Protestant and Protestant. This difference is between those who agree on justification by faith and nearly every other fundamental doctrine of the gospel.

If Christian differences are more in opinion than from real experience, and more in expression than in opinion, why do Christians so angrily contend with one another on this one point? Several reasons may be given. The main reason is their not understanding one another joined with pride of their opinions and also their particular modes of expression.

In order to remove some of this problem and attempt to aid our understanding one another on this point, I shall endeavor to show what is the righteousness of Christ; when, and in what sense, it is imputed to us, and then conclude with a short and plain application of it.

The Righteousness of Christ

The righteousness of Christ is twofold: His divine and His human righteousness.

His divine righteousness belongs to His divine nature, as He is. He that existed over all, God, blessed for ever, the supreme, the eternal, the Equal Father as regarding His Godhead, though inferior to the Father regarding His manhood. Now this is His eternal, essential, immutable holiness. It is His infinite justice, mercy and truth—in all which He and the Father are one.

But the divine righteousness of Christ is immediately concerned in the question before us. Few contend the imputation of His divine righteousness to us. Those who believe the doctrine of imputation understand this to be His human righteousness.

The human righteousness of Christ belongs to Him in His human nature. He is the mediator between God and man. This is either internal or external. His internal righteousness is the image of God, stamped on every power and faculty of His soul. It is a copy of His divine righteousness, so far as it can be imparted to a human spirit. It is a transcript of the divine purity, the divine justice, mercy, and truth. It includes love, reverence, resignation to His Father, with humility, meekness, gentleness, and love to lost mankind. It includes every other holy and heavenly temper, and all these in the highest degree, without any defect or mixture of unholiness.

The least part of His external righteousness was that He did nothing wrong. He knew no outward sin of any kind, He had no guile and He never spoke one improper word, nor did one improper action. This is only a negative righteousness which no one ever had nor ever can have except Jesus.

His outward righteousness was positive also. He did all things well. In every word of His tongue, in every work of His hands, He did precisely the will of God who sent Him. In the whole course of His life He did the Father's will on earth, just as it is done in heaven. All He acted and spoke was perfect for its circumstance. The whole and every part of His obedience was complete. "He fulfilled all righteousness."

But His obedience implied more than all this. It implied not only doing, but suffering. He suffered the whole will of God—from the time He came into the world until He bore our sins in His own body upon the cross; then having made a full atonement for our sins, He bowed His head and gave up the spirit. This is usually termed the passive righteousness of Christ. The former is His active righteousness. But the active and passive righteousness of Christ were never separated from each other. We never need separate them at all, either in speaking or even in thinking. With both these joined in Him, Jesus is "The Lord our Righteousness."

Christ's Righteousness Is Imparted

When is it that any of us may personally acclaim "The Lord our Righteousness?" In other words, when is it that the righteousness of Christ is imputed to us, and in what sense is it imputed?

Search the world and observe all those in it are either believers or unbelievers. Observe next without dispute, to all believers the righteousness of Christ is imputed. To unbelievers it is not.

When is it imputed? It is given when they believe. In that very moment, the righteousness of Christ is theirs. It is imputed to everyone who believes as soon as he believes. Faith and the righteousness of Christ are inseparable. If one believes according to Scripture, he believes in the righteousness of Christ. All true, saving faith has the righteousness of Christ for its object.

True, all believers may not speak the same, using the same language. That is not expected and we should not require it. Many circumstances may cause each to vary from the other in manner of expression. However, different expressions do not necessarily imply differences in sentiment. Different persons often use different expressions and yet mean the same thing. There is nothing unusual about this, although we seldom make allowance for it. It is not unusual for one, when speaking of the same subject at a considerable distance of time, to duplicate their expressions even though their sentiments are changed. How then can we be rigid in requiring others to use only our words and phrases?

Let us go a step further. Others may differ from us in their opinions, as well as in their expressions, and yet share with us our same saving faith. Possibly they do not have a clear understanding of the blessing which they enjoy. Their ideas may not be as clear as ours, yet their experience may be as genuine. There is a wide difference between the faculties of people and their understandings. That difference is greatly increased by education. This alone may be the reason for inconceivable differences in their opinions as well as expressions. Yet their hearts cleave to God through Christ, with a true interest in His righteousness.

Let us make all that allowance to others, which, were we in their place, we would ask for ourselves.

The sense in which this righteousness is imputed to believers is this: all believers are forgiven and accepted, not for the sake of anything in them or of anything that ever was, that is, or ever can be done by them, but wholly and solely for the sake of what Christ has done and suffered for them. "Not for works of righteousness which we have done, but of His own mercy He saved us." "By grace ye are saved, through faith, not of works lest any man should boast."

We are saved wholly and solely for the sake of what Christ has done and suffered for us. We are justified freely by His grace, and our redemption is in Jesus Christ. This is the only means of obtaining the favor of God and continuing in it. This is how we first come to God and it is the same way we come to Him ever after. We walk in one and the same new and living way until our spirit returns to God.

These words, and many others to the same effect, are extracted from the Homilies of The Church of England: "These things must necessarily go together in our justification: upon God's part, His great mercy and grace; upon Christ's part, the satisfaction of God's justice; and on our part, faith in the merits of Christ. So that the grace of God doth not shut out the righteousness of God in our justification, but only shutteth out the righteousness of man, as to deserving our justification." Also, "That we are justified by faith alone, is spoken to take away clearly all merit of our works, and wholly to ascribe the merit and deserving of our justification to Christ only. Our justification comes freely of the mere mercy of God, for whereas all the world was not able to pay any part towards our ransom, it pleased him, without any of our deserving, to prepare for us Christ's body and blood, whereby our ransom might be paid, and his justice satisfied. Christ, therefore, is now the righteousness of all them that truly believe in him."

The hymns I published speak the same. To cite all the passages to this effect would be to transcribe a great part of the volumes. One verse expresses all,

> "Jesus, thy blood and righteousness
> My beauty are, my glorious dress:
> 'Midst flaming worlds in these array'd,
> With joy shall I lift up my head."

In my sermon on justification, I express the same thing in these words: "In consideration of this, that the Son of God hath 'tasted death for every man,' God hath now 'reconciled the world unto himself, not imputing to them their former trespasses.' So that for the sake of his well-beloved Son, of what he hath done and suffered for us, God now vouchsafes, on only one condition (which He also enables us to perform), both to remit the punishment due to our sins, to reinstate us in his favor, and to restore our dead souls to spiritual life, as the earnest of life eternal."

Perhaps some will object, "But you affirm that faith is imputed to us for righteousness." Paul affirms this over and over, therefore I affirm it too. Faith is imputed for righteousness to every believer. This is faith in the righteousness of Christ, but this is exactly the same thing which has been said before. By that expression, I mean neither more nor less than that we are justified by faith, not by works. Every believer is forgiven and accepted, merely for the sake of what Christ has done and suffered.

Undoubtedly, a believer is invested or clothed with the righteousness of Christ. And accordingly, the use above recited is the language of every believing heart, "Jesus, thy blood and righteousness, My beauty are, my glorious dress." For the sake of His active and passive righteousness, I am forgiven and accepted of God.

Christ's Work, Not Ours

We must put off the filthy rags of our own imagined righteousness before we can put on the spotless righteousness of Christ. In plain terms, we must repent before we can believe the gospel. We must be cut off from any dependence upon ourselves before we can truly depend upon Christ. We must cast away all confidence in our own supposed righteousness or we cannot have a true confidence in His. Till we are delivered from trusting in anything that we do, we cannot thoroughly trust in what He has done and suffered. First, we receive the sentence of death in ourselves, then we trust in Him who lived and died for us.

Also I believe in inherent righteousness, in its proper place. This is not the ground of our acceptance with God, but is the fruit of it. It is not in place of imputed righteous-

ness, but a result of it. That is, God implants righteousness in everyone to whom he has imputed it. Christ Jesus
is made by God unto us sanctification as well as righteousness. God sanctifies, as well as justifies, all who believe in
Him. Those to whom the righteousness of Christ is imputed, are made righteous by the Spirit of Christ. They
are renewed in the image of God, which "is created in
righteousness and true holiness."

Do we put faith in place of Christ or of His righteousness? By no means. I take particular care to put each of
these in its proper place. We do not have faith in faith.
The righteousness of Christ is the whole and sole foundation of all our hope. It is by faith we are enabled to build
upon this foundation. God gives this faith. At the moment
we are accepted of God we receive faith, not for the sake
of that faith, but for what Christ has done and suffered
for us. Each of these has its proper place, and neither
clashes with the other. We believe, we love, we endeavor
to walk blameless in all the commandments of the Lord.

Therefore, I no more deny the righteousness of Christ
than I deny the Godhead of Christ. No one may charge me
with denying either one or the other. Neither do I deny
imputed righteousness. I continually affirm that the righteousness of Christ is imputed to every believer.

But who does deny this? All infidels, whether baptized
or unbaptized, who say the glorious gospel of our Lord
Jesus Christ is only a fable. All who deny the supreme
Godhead of the Lord, supposing Him to be a mere creature
of consequence, deny His divine righteousness. They also
deny His human righteousness, as imputed to any man,
because they believe everyone is accepted for his own efforts and good works.

The human righteousness of Christ, at least the imputation of it, as the whole and sole meritorious cause of
the justification of a sinner before God, is similarly denied

by the members of the church of Rome, if they are true to their doctrines. Undoubtedly there are many Catholics whose experience goes beyond their doctrines. Although their conceptions of this great truth be incomplete, yet they believe in their hearts. They trust in Christ alone, and not their church, both for their present and eternal salvation.

In the Protestant churches, those who are usually termed Mystics often trust in their own efforts. It is well known that many of these absolutely and zealously deny the imputation of the righteousness of Christ, as zealously as Robert Barclay, who dared to say, "Imputed righteousness—imputed nonsense!" The people known by the name of Quakers espouse the same sentiment. Most of those who profess themselves members of the church are totally ignorant of the matter and know nothing about imputed righteousness. Some see this, together with justification by faith, as being destructive to good works. To these we may add a considerable number of people from other denominations. I am not called to pass judgment and I leave this to Him who made them. I "dare" not say that all who are not clear in their opinions or expressions are void of all Christian experience. No one says they are all in a state of damnation, without hope, without God in the world, however confused their ideas may be or however improper their language. There are many of them whose heart is right toward God and who effectually know The Lord our Righteousness.

Blessed be God, all are not among those who are dim in their conceptions and expressions. Let them use any expressions they believe to be more exactly scriptural, provided their hearts rest only on what Christ has done and suffered—for pardon, grace, and glory. I cannot express this better than in Hervey's words which are worthy to be written in letters of gold. "We are not solicitous as to any particular set of phrases. Only let men be humbled as repenting criminals at Christ's feet, let them rely as devoted pensioners on his merits, and they are undoubtedly in the way to a blessed immortality." There is no need and no possibility of saying more. We shall not wrangle. A man of peace here proposes terms of accommodation to all the contending parties.

The Truth Perverted

In the meantime, we are afraid that use of the phrase, "the righteousness of Christ" or "the righteousness of Christ is imputed to me," will be used as a cover for unrighteousness. We have seen this done numerous times. Reprove a person for drunkenness, as an example. "Oh," says he, "I pretend to no righteousness of my own; Christ is my righteousness." Another has been told that the extortioner and the unjust shall not inherit the kingdom of God. He replies with all assurance, "I am unjust in myself, but I have a spotless righteousness in Christ." This is the result. A person being far from the practice and the tempers of a Christian, neither with the mind which was in Christ nor walking as He walked, shields himself against conviction by what he calls the righteousness of Christ.

It is seeing so many deplorable instances of this kind which causes us to sparingly use these grand expressions. I call upon all of you who use these frequently and beg you in the name of Christ; earnestly guard all that hear you against this accursed abuse. Warn all against "continuing in sin that grace may abound." Warn them against making Christ the minister of sin. Do not nullify that solemn decree of God, "Without holiness no man shall see the Lord," by any vain imagination of being holy in Christ! Warn them that if they remain unrighteous, the righteousness of Christ will profit them nothing! Cry aloud that for this very end the righteousness of Christ is imputed to us, so the righteousness of the law may be fulfilled in us and then we may live soberly, righteously, and godly in this present world.

Finally, let me make a short and clear application. First, would I condemn all that use them? That is bending the bow too much the other way. You should not condemn all who do not speak just as you do. You should not quarrel with those who use phrases they like, any more than they with you for doing the same. If they do quarrel with you upon that account, do not imitate their bigotry. Allow them the liberty which they should allow you. Never be angry at an expression simply because it has been abused. What expression has not? The abuse may be removed, while allowing the use to remain. Above all, be sure to retain the important sense which is in the expression. All the blessings I enjoy are given wholly and solely for the sake of what Christ has done and suffered for me.

Next, I add a few words to you who are fond of these expressions. Do I constrain you? Would you constrain me? Teach the whole sense for which you contend. We receive every blessing through the righteousness of God our Savior. I allow you to use whatever expressions you choose, asking only your guarding them against abuse. You are as deeply concerned to prevent it as I am. I frequently use the expression imputed righteousness. I often put this and the similar expressions before a whole congregation. Allow me liberty of conscience in it. Allow me the right of my own judgment. Allow me to use it just as often as I judge it preferable to any other expression, and be not angry with me if I cannot judge it proper to use any one expression every two minutes. Do as you please, but do not condemn me if I do not follow. For this, do not call me an enemy to the righteousness of Christ. Bear with me as I do with you, so we may fulfill the law of Christ. Do not make tragical outcries as though I were subverting the very foundations of Christianity. Whoever does this, does me much wrong.

I lay, and have done for many years, this one foundation. Indeed, "Other foundation can no man lay than that which is laid, even Jesus Christ." I build inward and outward holiness on this only by faith. If there is a difference of opinion, where is our Christianity if we cannot think and let think? Will you forgive me as as I forgive you? Why have a dispute about whether a particular mode of expression shall be used more or less frequently? We must earnestly be seeking to contend with each other if we can make this a bone of contention! Let us not contend any more. Such trifles as these give our common enemies room to criticize us and our religion.

Let us at length join hearts and hands in the service of our great Master. As we have one Lord, one faith, one hope of our calling, let us all strengthen each other's hands in God, and with one heart and one mouth declare to all mankind, "The Lord Our Righteousness."

4

*The Purpose of Christ's Coming**

For this purpose the Son of God was manifested, that he might destroy the works of the devil. (1 John 3:8)

Many eminent writers, both Christian and non-Christian, in all ages, have used their utmost talents in painting the beauty of virtue. They have taken the same pains to vividly describe the deformity of vice in general, as well as vices which were most prevalent in their respective ages and countries. With equal care they have shown the happiness that accompanies virtue, and the misery that usually accompanies vice and always follows it. Writings of this kind are certainly useful. Because of these writings, some probably have been stirred up to desire and follow after virtue. On the other hand, some may have been checked in their career of vice and perhaps been reclaimed from it, at least for a while. But changes effected in humans by these efforts is seldom either deep or universal—much less is it durable. In a little while it van-

---

Op. cit., Sermon LXVII, Vol. 2, pp. 67–73.

ishes away as the morning mist. Simple motives are far too feeble to overcome the countless temptations which surround us. All that can be said of the beauty and advantage of virtue and the deformity and ill effects of vice are never enough to overcome and heal one irregular appetite or passion.

There is an absolute necessity, if we plan to conquer vice or steadily persevere in the practice of virtue, to have stronger weapons. Otherwise, while we may see what is right, we cannot attain it. Many thoughtful men, even among the irreligious, have been deeply aware of this. Even the Roman philosophers could discover the impotence of the human mind. "There is in every man," one said, "this weakness, the thirst for glory." Nature points out the disease, but nature shows us no remedy.

It is not strange they found no remedy, although they sought for one. They sought the remedy where it never was and never will be found—in themselves, in reason, and in philosophy. They did not seek it in God. In Him alone it is possible to find it. In God? No! They totally disclaim this solution in the strongest terms. For although Cicero, a Roman oracle, once stumbled upon that strange truth, "There never was any great man who was not divinely inspired," yet in the very same tract he contradicted himself. He totally overthrew his own assertion by asking, "Who ever returned thanks to God for his virtue or wisdom?" A Roman poet, after mentioning several outward blessings, honestly adds, "We ask of God what He can give or take—life, wealth; but virtuous I myself will make."

The best of them either sought virtue partly from God and partly from themselves, or sought it from those gods who were only devils and not likely to make any petitioners better than themselves. This dimness was the light of the wisest of men until life and immortality were brought

to light by the gospel and the Son of God was manifested
to destroy the works of the devil.

The Works of the Devil

What are the works of the devil mentioned in this
scripture? How was the Son of God manifested to destroy
those works? In what manner, through what steps, does
Jesus actually destroy them? These three very important
points will now be discussed.

What these works of the devil are, we learn from the
words preceding and following the text, "Ye know that he
was manifested to take away our sins. Whosoever abideth
in him, sinneth not: whosoever sinneth, hath not seen Him
neither knoweth him. . . . He that committeth sin is of the
devil; for the devil sinneth from the beginning. For this
purpose the Son of God was manifested, that he might
destroy the works of the devil. Whosoever is born of God
doth not commit sin."

From the whole of this it is clear that the works of the
devil are sin and the fruits of sin.

The wisdom of God has now evaporated the clouds of
ignorance which so long covered the earth and put an end
to childish conjectures concerning these things. So now we
can take a more distinct view of these works of the devil,
so far as the Scriptures instruct us. The work of the Holy
Spirit was to assist our faith, not gratify our curiosity.
Therefore, the account He has given (the first chapters of
Genesis) is very short. Nevertheless, it is so clear we may
learn from it whatever He wants us to know.

We may review the matter from the beginning. "The
Lord God created man in His own image"—in His own
natural image. His image is spirit, as God is a spirit. Included is understanding. If that is not the essence of spirit,
it seems to be the most essential property of a spirit. Prob-

ably the human spirit, like the angelic, first discerned truth through intuition. Therefore Adam named every creature as soon as he saw it, according to its inmost nature. But Adam's knowledge was limited because he was a creature. Ignorance was inseparable from him, while error was not. It does not appear that he was mistaken in anything, but he was capable of mistake and of being deceived.

He was also endowed with a will and with various affections. He could love, desire, and delight in that which is good, otherwise his understanding had no purpose. He was also given a free will, the power of choosing what was good and rejecting what was not. Without this, both the will and the understanding would have been utterly useless; man would have been far from being a free agent, being no agent at all. Every unfree being is purely passive—not active in any degree. Imagine a sword in your hand. If a man stronger than you seizes your hand and forces you to wound a third person, you are no more an agent than the sword. The hand is as passive as the blade. So in every possible case, one who is not free is not an agent but a patient.

It seems, therefore, that every spirit in the universe is endowed with understanding, with a will, and with a measure of freedom. These three are inseparably united in every intelligent nature. Remember, however, a free will overruled is really no free will at all. Such is a contradiction in terms. It is the same as unfree freedom, which is downright nonsense.

It may be further observed that where there is no free will, there can be no moral good or evil, no virtue or vice. The fire warms us, yet it is not capable of virtue. It burns us, yet this is no vice. There is no virtue except when an intelligent being knows, loves, and chooses what is good. There is no vice except when such a being knows, loves, and chooses what is evil.

So, God created man not only in His natural image, but likewise in His own moral image. He created him not only in knowledge, but also in righteousness and true holiness. As his understanding was without blemish—perfect in its kind—so were all his affections. They were all set right and focused on their proper objectives. As a free agent, Adam steadily chose whatever was good, according to the direction of his understanding. In doing so he was completely happy, dwelling in God and God in him. He had uninterrupted fellowship with the Father and the Son through the eternal Spirit and the continual testimony of his conscience that all his ways were good and acceptable to God.

Yet free will necessarily included a power of choosing good or evil. Some have questioned whether Adam could even choose evil, not knowing what it was. No doubt, he could *mistake* evil or good. He was not infallible, therefore he was not impeccable. This unravels the whole difficulty of the great question of how evil came into the world. Evil came from "Lucifer, son of the morning." It was the work of the devil. He was the first sinner in the universe, the author of sin, the first being who, by the abuse of his free will, introduced evil into the creation. He was tempted to think too highly of himself. He freely yielded to the temptation and gave way, first to pride, then to self-will. He said, "I will sit upon the mount of the congregation, in the sides of the north; I will ascend above the heights of the clouds: I will be like the Most High." He did not fall alone, but soon drew after him a third part of the angels of heaven, in consequence of which they lost their glory and happiness and were driven from their habitation.

Having great envy with its resulting wrath at the happiness of the creatures God had newly created, it is not strange Satan would desire and work to take happiness from them. In order to do this, he concealed himself as the serpent, who was the most subtle or intelligent of all the brute creatures. On that account the serpent was the least likely to raise suspicion. Indeed, some don't believe the serpent was then clothed with reason and speech. If he weren't, why did Eve have conversation with him? She would have been frightened rather than deceived. To deceive her, Satan mingled truth with falsehood.

"Hath God said, Ye may not eat of every tree of the garden?" Soon after he persuaded her to disbelieve God, to imagine His threats would not be fulfilled. She then became open to the whole temptation, to the desire of the flesh, for the tree was good for food. Then came the desire of the eyes, for it was pleasant to the eyes, and also to the pride of life, for it could make one wise and consequently honored. Thus unbelief begot pride. Eve thought herself wiser than God and capable of finding a better way to happiness than God had taught. From this emerged her self-will. She was determined to do her own will, not the will of God. Her foolish desires completed all this in the outward sin when she took the fruit and ate it.

She then gave the fruit to her husband and he also ate. At that moment he died. The life of God was extinguished in his soul. God's glory departed from him. He lost the whole moral image of God—His righteousness and true holiness. He was now unholy, unhappy, full of sin, full of guilt, and full of tormenting fears. Being broken off from God, now seeing Him as an angry Judge, Adam was afraid. His confused understanding was demonstrated when he thought he could hide himself from the presence of the Lord. His soul was now utterly dead to God. Likewise, on that day his body began to die. It became subject to weakness, sickness, and pain, preparatory to the death of the body and eternal death. These are the works of the devil, sin and its fruits, considered in their order. Now we may see how the Son of God was manifested to destroy those works.

Jesus Came to Restore Life

Jesus was manifested as the only begotten Son of God, in glory equal with the Father, to the inhabitants of heaven, before and at the foundation of the world. The universal belief of the ancient church was that none had seen God the Father and from all eternity He had dwelt in unapproachable light. Only in and by the Son of His love had He revealed himself to His creatures.

How Jesus was manifested to Adam and Eve in paradise is not easy to determine. It is generally supposed He appeared to them in the form of a man and conversed with them face to face.

We reasonably believe it was by similar appearances that He was manifested in succeeding ages to Enoch, while he walked with God. Later He was manifested to Noah before and after the deluge, to Abraham, Isaac and Jacob on various occasions, and to mention no more, to Moses: This seems to be the obvious meaning of the words, "My servant Moses . . . is faithful in all mine house. With him will I speak mouth to mouth, even apparently, and not in dark speeches; and the similitude of the Lord shall he behold," namely the Son of God.

But all these were only types of His great manifestation. It was in God's time that the Father "sent forth his Son, made of a woman," by the power of the Spirit overshadowing her. Jesus was afterward manifested to the shepherds, to devout Simeon, Anna the prophetess, and to all who waited for redemption in Jerusalem.

When Jesus was of age for executing His priestly office, He was manifested to Israel, preaching the gospel of the kingdom of God in every town and in every city. For a time He was glorified by all, who acknowledged that He spoke as no man ever spoke. He spoke as one having authority, with all the wisdom of God and the power of God. He was manifested by countless signs and wonders and mighty works, as well as by His whole life. He was the only one born of a woman who knew no sin and who from His birth to His death did all things well, continually doing not His own will but the will of Him who sent Him.

"Behold the Lamb of God, which taketh away the sin of the world!" This was a more glorious manifestation of himself than any He had made before. How wonderfully He was manifested to angels and men, when He was wounded for our transgressions and when He bore all our sins in His own body on the cross. Having, by that one offering of himself, made a full and perfect satisfaction for the sins of the whole world, He lovingly cried out, "It is finished," and bowed His head and gave up the spirit.

We need to mention further manifestations: His resurrection from the dead, His ascension into heaven and the glory which He had before the world began, and His pouring out the Holy Spirit on the Day of Pentecost. This is beautifully described in the words of the Psalmist, "Thou hast ascended on high, thou hast led captivity captive: thou hast received gifts for men; yea, for the rebellious also that the Lord God might dwell among [or in] them."

"That the Lord God might dwell in them" refers to a still further manifestation of the Son of God—His inward manifestation of himself. When Jesus spoke of this to His apostles, one immediately asked, "Lord, how is it that thou wilt manifest thyself unto us, and not unto the world?" This comes by His enabling us to believe in His name. Jesus is inwardly manifested to us when we are enabled to confidently say, "My Lord, and my God!" Then each of us can boldly say, "The life which I now live in the flesh I live by the faith of the Son of God, who loved me, and gave himself for me." It is by His manifesting himself in our hearts that He effectually destroys the works of the devil.

We need to consider how He does this, in what manner, and by what steps He actually destroys them. First, as Satan began his first work in Eve by tainting her with unbelief, so Jesus begins His work in man by enabling us to believe in Him. He both opens and enlightens our eyes of understanding. Out of the darkness He commands light to shine and takes away the veil which Satan had spread over our hearts. We then see, not by reasoning but by a kind of revelation and in a direct way, that "God was in Christ reconciling the world unto himself, not imputing their trespasses unto them," not imputing them to me.

When that happens we know we are of God, children of God by faith, having redemption through the blood of Christ and forgiveness of sins. Having experienced justification by faith, we have peace with God through our Lord Jesus Christ. That peace enables us in every state to be content, delivers us from all perplexing doubts, from all tormenting fears, and, in particular, from fear of death, to which we were subject all our life.

At the same time, Christ strikes at the root of that grand work of the devil, pride, causing the sinner to humble himself before the Lord and abhor himself, as it were, in dust and ashes. Jesus strikes at the root of self-will, enabling the humbled sinner to say in all things, "Not as I will, but as God wills." He destroys the love of the world, delivering them who believe in Him from every foolish and harmful desire—from the desire of the flesh, the desire of the eyes, and the pride of life.

He saves them from seeking or expecting to find happiness in any creature. As Satan turned the heart of man from the Creator to the creature, the Son of God turns his heart back again, from the creature to the Creator. Thus, by manifesting himself, He destroys the works of the devil, restoring the guilty outcast from God back to His favor, for pardon and peace. The sinner, in whom dwelt no good thing, is given to love and holiness. The burdened and miserable sinner receives unspeakable joy and real, substantial happiness.

But it must be observed, Christ does not destroy the whole work of the devil in man, as long as man remains in this life. Jesus does not yet destroy human weakness, sickness, pain, and a thousand infirmities inherent to the flesh. He does not destroy all that weakness of understanding which is the natural consequence of the soul's dwelling in a corruptible body. Remaining still are both ignorance and error, which belong to humanity. He entrusts us with only a very small share of knowledge in our present state, lest our knowledge should interfere with our humility, and we should again seek to be like God. It is to remove from us all temptation to pride and all thought of independence that He leaves us with these infirmities, particularly the weakness of understanding, until our final sentence takes place, "Dust thou art, and unto dust shalt thou return!"

At death, error, pain, and all bodily infirmities cease. Death itself, "the last enemy" of man, shall be destroyed at the resurrection. The moment we hear the voice of the archangel and the trump of God, "then shall be brought to pass the saying that is written, Death is swallowed up in victory." This corruptible body shall put on incorruption, this mortal body shall put on immortality, and the Son of God, manifested in the clouds of heaven, shall destroy this last work of the devil.

Here also, we see real Christianity in the clearest, strongest light—Christ's restoration of man to all he has been deprived of by Satan. True religion restores us not only to the favor but to the image of God. The renewed person is not simply delivered from sin, but is also filled with the fullness of God. It is obvious, if we attend to the preceding considerations, Christianity is nothing short of this. Everything else, whether negative or external, misses the mark. But what a paradox this is! How little it is understood in the Christian world, even in our enlightened age. Among all our wise discoveries, who has discovered this? How few, either educated or uneducated. Yet, if we believe the Bible, who can deny it? Who can doubt it? It runs through the Bible from the beginning to the end in one connected chain. The agreement of every part of the Bible is the analogy of faith. Beware of taking anything else or anything less than this for Christianity! Do not imagine an outward form or any round of duties, either public or private, is Christianity. Least of all dream that orthodoxy and right opinion is faith. Of all religious dreams, this is the vainest.

Do not take anything less than this for the religion of Jesus Christ. Do not accept a part of it in place of the whole! What God has joined together, put not asunder. Take no less for His religion than the faith that works by love all inward and outward holiness. Do not be content with any religion which does not imply the destruction of all the works of the devil—sin.

We know incomplete understanding and a thousand infirmities will remain while this corruptible body remains, but sin need not remain. Sin is the work of the devil, eminently so called, which the Son of God was manifested to destroy in this present life. He is able, He is willing, to destroy it now, in all who believe in Him. Do not distrust His power or His love. He has spoken and He is ready to perform. Come boldly to the throne of grace, trusting in His mercy, and you shall find, "He saveth to the uttermost all those that come to God through Him." Ask Jesus to give you His true religion with freedom from sin. Put His promises to the proof. Let Him destroy the works of the devil in your life.

5

*The Circumcision of the Heart**

Circumcision is that of the heart, in the spirit, and not in the letter. (Romans 2:29)

A good man recently remarked that anyone now preaching true Christianity is in danger of being called a heretic. Most professing Christians live so differently from Christ that as soon as any of Christ's truths are shown which are different from the spirit of the world, so-called Christians object, "You teach strange things. What do you mean?" This is an odd reaction to one who is only preaching Jesus and the resurrection, with the necessary consequences. *If Christ has risen, you ought to die to the world and live wholly unto God.*

This is a hard demand to the natural man, one who is alive to the world and dead to God. This person will not easily receive the truth of God, unless it is so watered down in the interpretation as to have neither use nor significance remaining. So he accepts none of the words of God in their plain and obvious meaning. They are foolish-

---

Op. cit., Sermon XVIII, Vol. 1, pp. 147–153.

ness to him. He cannot understand them because they are spiritually discerned. They are perceivable only by a spiritual sense which was never awakened in him. Lacking perception, he must reject as idle fancies of men, both the wisdom and the power of God.

Circumcision of the Heart

So a circumcision of the heart—in spirit and not in letter—is a distinguishing mark of the true follower of Christ. This is neither outward circumcision nor baptism nor any other outward religious form; it is a right state of soul, with one's mind and spirit renewed after the image of Him who created it. This is a great truth that can only be spiritually discerned. Paul shows this in the next words, "whose praise is not of men, but of God." It is as if he had said, "Don't expect to follow your great Master and have the world. The circumcision of the heart, the Christian seal of understanding, is foolishness to the world. Be content to wait for your praise until the day of Jesus' coming. On that day, you shall have praise from God, in the grand assembly of men and angels."

Now, let us inquire about the nature of the circumcision of the heart. In general we may observe circumcision of the heart is that habitual disposition of soul which the Bible terms holiness. This directly implies being cleansed from sin, "from all filthiness of the flesh and spirit." By consequence, one is endued with those virtues which were in Christ Jesus. It is being so renewed in the spirit of our mind as to be perfect as our Father in heaven is perfect.

To be more specific, circumcision of the heart implies humility, faith, hope, and charity. Humility, the honest judgment of ourselves, cleanses our minds from high conceits about our perfections. It removes our unduly high opinion of our own abilities and attainments. Such conceits are the genuine fruit of a corrupted nature. Humility entirely cuts off the vain thought, "I am rich and wise, and have need of nothing." It convinces us that in and of ourselves we are "wretched, and miserable, and poor, and blind, and naked." It convinces us that even at our best, we are, of ourselves, all sin and vanity. Confusion, ignorance, and error constantly reign over us. In a word, in man there is no good part in our soul and the foundations of human nature are out of plumb.

At the same time, we are convinced we are not able, of ourselves, to help ourselves. Without the Spirit of God we can do nothing but add sin to sin. He alone, who works in us by His almighty power, is able to will and to do that which is good. It is impossible for us even to think a good thought without the supernatural assistance of His Spirit to renew our souls in righteousness and true holiness.

The effect, once we recognize our own sinfulness and helplessness, is to disregard all praise and honor which comes from man, that praise which is usually given for some supposed excellence in us. He who knows himself neither desires nor values the applause which he knows he does not deserve. Therefore it is not important for him to be judged by man's judgment. He has reason to think, by comparing what has been said—either for or against him—with what he feels in his own heart. He knows the world, as well as Satan, was a liar from the beginning. And even as to those who are Christians, he would choose for them to judge him only as one desiring to be a faithful steward of his Lord's goods. Hopefully, this might be a means of enabling him to be of more use to his fellow man. He is assured that whatever God wills for him will be followed by the grace to perform it. He is always able through God's grace.

This is that meekness which those who follow His example and tread in His steps have learned of Christ. This knowledge of their sinful condition, and the subsequent cleansing from pride and vanity, allows them to embrace with a willing mind the second thing implied in circumcision of heart. That is faith, which alone is able to make us whole, the one medicine given by heaven to heal spiritual sickness.

The Importance of Faith

The best guide of the blind, the surest light for those who are in darkness, and the most perfect instructor of the foolish is faith. This must be a faith that is mighty through God, capable of pulling down Satan's strongholds. Such a faith overturns all the prejudices of our corrupt reason, all the false maxims revered among men, all evil customs and habits, and all that wisdom of the world which is foolishness with God. Faith casts down imaginations, reasonings, and everything that exalts itself against the knowledge of God. It brings into captivity every thought to the obedience of Christ.

"All things are possible to him that believeth." The spiritual eyes of our understanding being enlightened, we see our only calling. It is to glorify God, who has bought us with a high price. Our body and spirit are now God's by redemption, as well as by creation. With this comes the feeling of God's great power—He who raised up Christ from the dead is able to raise us who are dead in sin.

This is the victory which overcomes the world, our faith—the faith *which is an unshaken assent to all that God has revealed in Scripture.*

In particular, faith confirms those important truths, "Christ Jesus came into the world to save sinners," "[He] bore our sins in his own body on the tree," "He is the propitiation for our sins, and not for ours only, but also for the sins of the whole world."

Likewise, the revelation of Christ comes into our hearts. There is a divine evidence or conviction of His love—His free, unmerited love to me, a sinner—and a sure confidence in His pardoning mercy wrought in us by the Holy Spirit. By this confidence every true believer is enabled to bear witness, "I know that my Redeemer liveth," that I have an "advocate with the Father," and that "Jesus Christ the righteous" is my Lord, and "the propitiation for our sins." It is now known He has loved me, and given himself for me. He has reconciled me, even me, to God, and I have redemption through His blood and forgiveness of my sins.

Such a faith as this cannot fail to show the power of Him who inspires it, by delivering His children from the bondage of sin while purging their consciences from dead works. It strengthens them so they are no longer bound to obey sin and its desires. Instead of yielding to it, they now yield themselves entirely to God, being alive from the dead.

Hope Is Born

Those who are thus by faith born of God, also have strong comfort through hope. This is the next thing which the circumcision of the heart implies. It is the testimony of their own spirit with God's which witnesses in their hearts that they are the children of God. It is the same Spirit who witnesses in them the clear and cheerful confidence that their hearts are upright toward God. It gives the good assurance that they now do, through His grace, the things which are acceptable in His sight and they are now in the path which leads to life. By the mercy of God they shall endure in that path to the end. It is He who gives them a lively expectation of receiving all good things from God's hand, including a joyous prospect of the crown of glory which is reserved in heaven for them. This anchor keeps a Christian steady in the midst of the storms of this troubled world and preserves him from floundering on either of those fatal rocks: presumption or despair. He is not discouraged by a misconceived severity of his Lord nor does he belittle His mercy. He neither believes the difficulties of the race set before him are greater than he has strength to conquer nor does he expect them to be so small that he never has to put forth all his strength. Experiences he already has in Christian warfare assure him his labor is not in vain, if he does with all his might whatever he finds to do. It forbids his believing that he can gain any advantage, and virtue, any praise, with a faint heart and feeble hands. He expects to pursue the same course as Paul, the great apostle of the Gentiles. "I," said Paul, "so run, not as uncertainly; so fight I, not as one that beateth the air: but I keep under my body, and bring it into subjection: lest that by any means, when I have preached to others, I myself should be a castaway."

By the same discipline, every good soldier of Christ is to inure himself to endure hardship. Confirmed and strengthened by faith, not only will he be able to renounce the works of darkness, but also every appetite and every affection not subject to the laws of God. "Every man," said John, "that hath this hope in him purifieth himself even as he is pure." It is his daily care, by the grace of God in Christ, to purge the inmost recesses of his soul from the lusts that before possessed and defiled it, always seeking removal of uncleanness, envy, malice, wrath, and every passion and temper that is from the flesh, that either springs from or cherishes his natural corruption. He whose body is the temple of God ought to admit into it nothing that is unclean, so holiness adorns that house forever where the Spirit of holiness dwells.

Loving God

A deep humility, a steadfast faith, a lively hope, and a cleansed heart leave one void of inbred pollution. If you will be perfect, add to all these charity. Add love and you have the circumcision of the heart. Love is the fulfilling of the law, the end of the commandment. Wonderful things are spoken about love. It is the essence, the spirit, the life of all virtue. It is not only the first and great command, but it is all the commandments in one. Whatever is just, whatever is pure, whatever is amiable or honorable, and if there is any virtue, if there is any praise, they are all comprised in this one word: love. In this is perfection and glory and happiness. The royal law of heaven and earth is this, "Thou shalt love the Lord thy God with all thy heart, and with all thy soul, and with all thy mind, and with all thy strength."

This does not forbid us to love anything besides God. It implies that we love our brother also. Nor does it forbid us, as some have thought, to have any pleasure in anything but God. To suppose this is to suppose the source of holiness is directly the cause of sin, since He has inseparably attached pleasure to the use of all things necessary to sustain the life He has given us. Therefore, this can never be the meaning of His command. The real meaning, both Jesus and His apostles frequently tell us, is so obvious as to not be misunderstood. "The Lord our God is one Lord," "Thou shalt have no other gods before me," "Thou shalt love the Lord thy God with all thy strength," "cleave unto Him," and "The desire of our soul is to thy name." It is no other than this. The one perfect good shall be your one ultimate end. One thing shall you desire for its own sake, the fruition of Him. That is all in all. The only happiness you shall propose to your souls is a union with Him who made you. This is the fellowhip with the

Father and the Son, and being joined to the Lord in one spirit. One goal you are to pursue to the end of time, the enjoyment of God in time and in eternity.

Desire other things if they tend to this. Love the creature, as that leads to the Creator. But in every step you take, let this be the glorious point that terminates your view. Let every affection, thought, word, and work be subordinate to this. Whatever you desire or fear, whatever you seek or shun, whatever you think, speak or do, let it be to order your happiness in God as the sole end as well as the source of your being.

There is no ultimate end but God. Jesus said one thing is needed, and if your eye is singly fixed on this one thing, your whole body shall be full of light. Paul expressed it, "This one thing I do. . . . I press toward the mark for the prize of the high calling of God in Christ Jesus." James agreed, "Cleanse your hands, ye sinners, and purify your hearts, ye double minded." John added, "Love not the world, neither the things that are in the world. . . . For all that is in the world, the lust of the flesh, and the lust of the eye, and the pride of life, is not of the Father, but is of the world."

Seeking happiness in what gratifies the desire of the flesh, the desire of the eye, or the pride of life is not from the Father. Those strivings come not from the Father but from the world. It is the distinguishing mark of those who will not have God reign over them.

We have particularly discussed what the circumcision of heart is, which will gain God's praise. Next, let us mention some reflections that naturally arise from this, and a plain rule whereby everyone may judge for himself whether he is of the world or of God.

The Uncircumcised Heart

It is clear from what has been said, that no man receives the praise of God unless his heart is circumcised by humility and he is little in his own eyes. He must be deeply convinced of the inbred corruption of his nature, knowing he is very far gone from original righteousness, being prone to all evil. Man has a carnal mind which is enmity against God and is not subject to the law of God. He can neither think, nor desire, nor speak, nor act anything good or well-pleasing in God's sight, except by His grace.

Thus, no man has a title to the praise of God until he feels his need of God and seeks that honor which comes only from God. God neither desires nor pursues what comes from man, unless it comes from His will.

Another truth, which naturally follows, is that no one shall obtain God's honor unless his heart is circumcised by faith—a faith of the operation of God. Refusing to be led any longer by his senses, appetites, or passions, or even by that blind leader of the blind so idolized by the world— natural reason—by faith he lives and walks. Such a person directs every step as seeing Him who is invisible, looking not at the temporal things which are seen but at the things which are not seen and are eternal. He governs all his desires, plans and thoughts, all his actions and conversations, as one who is next to Jesus, who sits at the right hand of God.

Our gospel knows no other foundation of good works than faith, faith in Christ. So, it clearly informs us that we are not Christians while we either deny Him to be the author or His Spirit to be the inspirer and perfecter of our faith and works.

"If any man have not the Spirit of Christ, he is none of his." He alone can quicken those who are dead to God. He alone can breathe into them the breath of Christian life and accompany and follow them with His grace, bringing their good desires to good effect. "As many as are thus led by the Spirit of God, they are the sons of God."

This is God's short and plain account of true religion

and virtue, and "other foundation can no man lay."

From what has been said, we may next learn that no one is truly led by the Spirit unless that Spirit bears witness with his spirit that he is a child of God, unless he sees the prize and crown before him and rejoices in hope of the grace of God. Many have erred by teaching that while serving God we ought not to have a view to our own happiness, but we are often and expressly taught of God to have respect for the recompense of reward and to balance the toil with the joy set before us. These light afflictions are followed with that "exceeding weight of glory." So we are aliens to the covenant of promise and are without God in the world, until God, in His abundant mercy, has given us a living hope of the incorruptible inheritance which is undefiled and does not fade away.

If these things are so, it is high time for all persons to deal faithfully with their own souls. Those who are far from finding themselves in this joyful assurance shall obtain the promises of that covenant when the terms are fulfilled. Quarreling with the covenant, blaspheming the terms of it, complaining of its severity, saying that no man ever did or shall live up to them, will not bring His grace. What is this but to reproach God, as if He were a hard master, requiring more of His servants than He enables them to perform? That makes Him appear as if He had mocked the helpless works of His hands by binding them to impossibilities and commanded them to overcome where neither their own strength nor His grace was sufficient.

Such blasphemy might almost persuade some to imagine themselves guiltless, while they are really hoping to fulfill the commands of God without any effort at all. Vain hope! No one should ever expect to see the kingdom of Christ and of God without striving, without agonizing first, to enter in at the narrow gate.

No one will ever be purified as the Lord is pure without treading in His steps and taking up His cross daily. And no one should ever dream of shaking off old opinions, passions, tempers, or of being sanctified throughout in spirit, soul and body, without a constant and continued course of general self-denial.

What less than this can we ever infer from those words of Paul, who lived "in infirmities, in reproaches, in necessities, in persecutions, in distresses" for Christ's sake? Paul, being full of signs and wonders and mighty deeds, having been caught up into the third heaven, worried that all his virtues would be insecure, and even his salvation in danger, without this constant self-denial.

"I therefore so run," wrote Paul, "not as uncertainly; so fight I, not as one that beateth the air." By this, he plainly teaches us that he who does not so run, who does not so deny himself daily, runs uncertainly, and fights to such little purpose that he beats the air.

There is little purpose fighting the fight of faith, vainly hoping to attain the crown of incorruption, when the heart is not circumcised by love. Love cuts off the lust of the flesh, the lust of the eye, and the pride of life. It engages the whole man—body, soul and spirit—in the ardent pursuit of that one object. This love is so essential to a child of God that without it whoever lives is still counted as dead by God.

"Though I speak with the tongues of men and of angels, and have not love, I am become as sounding brass, or a tinkling cymbal. And though I have the gift of prophecy, and understand all mysteries, and all knowledge, and though I have all faith, so that I could remove mountains, and have not love, I am nothing." Though I give all my money to feed the poor, and my body to be martyred, and have no love, it all profits me nothing.

Application

Here, then, is the sum of the perfect law, this is the true circumcision of the heart. Let the spirit return to God who gave it with this whole train of its affections. Unto the place from where all rivers came, let them flow there again. He does not need other sacrifices from us. It is the living sacrifice of the heart He has chosen. Let this be continually offered up to God through Christ in flames of holy love. He is a "jealous" God. He will not divide His throne with another. He must reign without a rival. No design, no desire may be admitted, but what has Him for its ultimate object.

Desire to live only to praise His name; let all your thoughts, words, and works tend to His glory. Set your heart firmly on Him, and other things only as they are in and from Him. Let your soul be filled with so entire a love of Him that you may love nothing but for His sake. Have a pure intention of heart, a steadfast regard to His glory in all your actions. Fix your eyes upon the blessed hope of your calling and make all the things of the world minister unto it. Then, and not until then, is the mind in us which was also in Christ Jesus. Then in every motion of the heart, in every word of our mouth, in every work of our hands, we pursue nothing but in relation to Him and in subordination to His pleasure. Then we will never think, speak, or act to fulfill our own will, but seek only the will of Him who sent us. In whatever we do, we must do all to the glory of God.

6

*The Great Privilege of Those Who Are Born of God**

Whosoever is born of God doth not commit sin. (1 John 3:9)

Many have believed that being born of God was the same as being justified, and the new birth and justification were only different terms denoting the same thing. Certainly, on the one hand, whoever is justified is also born of God. On the other hand, whoever is born of God is also justified. Both these gifts of grace are given to every believer in the same moment. At the moment one's sins are blotted out, he is also born again of God.

Though it is true that justification and the new birth are inseparable from each other, they are easily distinguished as not the same, but of different natures. Justification implies only a relative change. The new birth is a real change. God, in justifying us, does something *for* us. In begetting us again, he does the work *in* us. The first changes our outward relation to God—from enemies we

_____

Op. cit., Sermon XIX, Vol. 1, pp. 162–168.

become children. By the latter, our inmost souls are changed—from sinners we become saints. One restores us to the favor of God; the other to the image of God. The first takes away the guilt; the other takes away the power of sin. So, although they are joined together in time, they are of wholly distinct natures.

Not understanding the great difference between being justified and being born again has caused great confusion of thought in many who have attempted to explain this great privilege of the children of God—whoever is born of God does not commit sin.

The Meaning of Being Born Again

First we must consider the proper meaning of the expression, "whosoever is born of God." In general, from all the passages of the Bible where this expression occurs, we may learn that it implies a vast inward change, a change wrought in the soul by the operation of the Holy Spirit, a change in the whole manner of our existence. From the moment we are born of God, we live in quite another manner than we did before. We are, as it were, in another world.

The foundation and reason of the expression is easily understood. When we undergo this great change, we may be said to be born again because there is a close resemblance between the circumstances of the natural and the spiritual birth. Hence, the easiest way to understand the spiritual birth is to consider the circumstances of natural birth.

An unborn child has little to do with this visible world—without any knowledge, conception or idea of worldly things, being surrounded with utter darkness.

The reason he is a stranger to the visible world is not because he is far away—it surrounds him on every side—

but because a thick veil is between him and the world, through which he can discern nothing.

No sooner is the child born into the world than he exists in a quite different manner. He now feels the air with which he is surrounded and which pours into him from every side as fast as he alternately breathes it back to sustain the flame of life—increasing his strength, his motion and his feeling. All the bodily senses are awakened and furnished with their proper objectives.

His eyes perceive the light, allowing discovery of an infinite variety of things with which he was unacquainted. Each sense is focused upon objects suitable to it. By these inlets the soul has an open relationship with the visible world, and a growing knowledge of sensible things is acquired.

So it is with one who is born of God. Before that great change is wrought, although God is in all who live and move and have their being, we are not aware of God, do not feel, and have no inward consciousness of His presence. So, one does not perceive that divine breath of life, without which no one can subsist a moment nor be aware of any of the things of God. Those things make no impression upon the soul.

God is continually calling to us from on high, but our spiritual ears are so shut that the voice of the Lord is lost on us. We do not see the things of the Spirit of God. The eyes of our understanding are closed and utter darkness covers our whole soul. It is true we may have some faint dawnings of life, some small beginnings of spiritual motion, but as yet we have no spiritual senses capable of discerning spiritual objects. Consequently, we do not discern the things of the Spirit of God and cannot know them because they are spiritually discerned.

We have no knowledge of the invisible world and little awareness of it. Not because it is far off, for we are in the midst of it, encompassed by it. The other world, as we usually term it, is not far from every one of us. It is above and beneath and on every side. Only the natural man cannot discern it because he has no spiritual senses with which to discern the things of God. There is a thick veil interposed which the natural man does not know how to penetrate.

How our manner of existence is changed when we are born of God and of the Spirit! The whole soul becomes aware of God and we can say by experience, "Thou art about my bed, and about my path," "I feel thee in all my ways," "Thou besettest me behind and before, and layest Thy hand upon me." The Spirit or breath of God is immediately inspired, breathed into the newborn soul, and the same breath which comes from God returns to God. As it is continually received by faith, so it is continually rendered back by love, by prayer, by praise, by thanksgiving—love and praise and prayer being the breath of every soul which is truly born of God. By this new kind of spiritual respiration, spiritual life is not only sustained but increased day by day, together with spiritual strength and motion and sensation. All the senses of the soul are now awake and capable of discerning spiritual good and evil.

The eyes of our understanding are now open and we can see Him who is invisible. We experience the exceeding greatness of His power and of His love toward those who believe. The reborn sees God is merciful to him, a sinner, and knows he is reconciled through the Son of His love. Clear perception shows both the pardoning love of God and all His exceeding great and precious promises. "God, who commanded the light to shine out of darkness, hath shined," and now shines in the heart to enlighten him with the knowledge of the glory of God in the face of Jesus Christ. All darkness is now passed away and he abides in the light of God's presence.

The ears are opened and the voice of God no longer calls in vain. Hearing and obeying the heavenly calling, we know the voice of our Shepherd. All spiritual senses are now awakened and we discover the invisible world. Hence the heart knows more and more of the things which it could not conceive before rebirth. Now we know the peace of God, the joy in the Holy Spirit, the love of God which is shed abroad in the hearts of them that believe in Him through Christ Jesus. Thus the veil is removed which before interrupted the light and voice, the knowledge and love of God. All who are born of the Spirit dwell in love and dwell in God and God lives in them. Having considered the meaning of that expression, "Whosoever is born of God," we now discuss in what sense he "doth not commit sin."

How to Live Without Sinning

One who is so born of God continually receives into his soul the breath of life from God, the gracious influence of His Spirit, and continually renders it back. He believes and loves and by faith perceives the continual actings of God upon his spirit. By a kind of spiritual reaction he returns the grace he receives in unceasing love and praise and prayer. Not only does he not commit sin while in this condition, but so long as this "seed remaineth in him, he cannot sin, because he is born of God."

By sin, I here understand outward sin, according to the plain, common acceptance of the word—an actual voluntary breaking of the law, the revealed, written law of God, of any commandment of God, acknowledged to be such at the time it is transgressed. For "whosoever is born of God," *while he abides in faith and love*, and in the spirit of prayer and thanksgiving, not only does not but cannot commit sin. So long as he believes in God through Jesus and loves Him and is pouring out his heart before Him, he cannot voluntarily transgress any command of God, either by speaking or acting what he knows God has forbidden. So long as that new nature remains in him, his loving, praying, thankful faith compels him to refrain from whatever he knows to be an abomination in the sight of God.

But here a difficulty immediately appears, one that has appeared insurmountable to many and induced them to deny that plain assertion of John and to give up the privilege of the children of God.

It is clear that many who have been truly born of God, having the Spirit of God given to them, not only could but did commit sin, even gross, outward sin. They transgressed the laws of God, speaking or acting what they knew He had forbidden.

David was unquestionably born of God and anointed king over Israel. He knew in whom he believed, he was strong in faith, always giving glory to God. The Lord, David knew, is our Shepherd, therefore we can lack nothing. He shall feed us in green pastures and lead us forth beside the waters of comfort. Even in a walk through the valley of the shadow of death, we need fear no evil for He is with us. David was filled with such love it caused him to cry out, "I will love Thee, oh Lord, my strength. The Lord is my rock and my fortress . . . the horn of my salvation, and my high tower." He was a man of prayer, pouring out his soul before God in all circumstances of life, and was abundant with praises and thanksgiving. David declared, "His praise shall continually be in my mouth." "Thou art my God, and I will praise thee: thou art my God, I will exalt Thee." And yet David could and did commit the terrible sins of adultery and murder.

Even after the Holy Spirit was more extensively given, after life and immortality were brought to light by the gospel, we have many sad examples of the same kind. These were undoubtedly written for our spiritual instruction.

A disciple who sold all his possessions for the relief of the apostles and was surnamed by them, "Barnabas," meaning "son of consolation," was chosen out of all the disciples, with Paul at Antioch, to carry relief to the Christians still in Judea. On his return from Judea, Barnabas was, at the direction of the Holy Spirit, separated from the other prophets and teachers for the work God had called him. He was selected to accompany Paul among the Gentiles and to be his fellow laborer everywhere. Nevertheless, Barnabas later was in such sharp disagreement with Paul over whether or not they should have John Mark—who had deserted them in Pamphylia—accompany them once more, that he also deserted Paul and went with John to Cyprus. In doing this, he was violating the arrangement dictated by the Holy Spirit.

An instance even more astonishing than both these is given by Paul in his epistle to the Galatians. When Peter, the first of the apostles and one of the three most highly favored by his Lord, came to Antioch, Paul faced him and publicly opposed him. In a vision at Joppa God had taught Peter, "What God hath cleansed, that call not thou common." Peter, therefore, ate with the Gentiles, those heathens converted to the Christian faith. When Christian Jews arrived from Jerusalem, however, Peter separated himself from the Gentiles out of fear of the Jews. In front of all at Antioch, Paul challenged Peter, "If thou, being a Jew, livest after the manner of the Gentiles" (not regarding the ceremonial law of Moses), "why compellest thou the Gentiles to live as do the Jews?" Here is also plain, undeniable sin committed by Peter, who was undoubtedly born of God. How can this be reconciled with the assertion of John, if taken in the obvious literal meaning, that "Whosoever is born of God doth not commit sin"?

From long observation, my answer is that as long as he who is born of God keeps himself in faith, which he is able to do by the grace of God, Satan cannot touch him. But if he does not keep in faith, if he does not live in the faith, he may commit sin even as another man.

It is easy to understand how any child of God might be moved from his own steadfastness, and yet the great truth of God, declared by the Apostle John, remains steadfast and unshaken. One who does not "keep himself" by that grace of God which is sufficient for him will fall, step by step; first into negative, inward sin, by not stirring up the gift of God which is in him, by not watching unto prayer, and not pressing on to the mark of the prize of his high calling. He then falls into positive inward sin, inclining to wickedness with his heart, giving way to some evil desire or temper. Next he loses his faith, his sight of a pardoning God, and consequently his love of God. He becomes weak and like any other man, and then is capable of committing even outward sin.

To explain this by a particular instance, David was born of God and saw God by faith. He loved God sincerely. He could truly say, "Whom have I in heaven but thee? and there is none upon earth [neither person nor thing] that I desire beside thee!" Still, there remained in his heart that corruption of nature which is the seed of all evil.

David was walking upon the roof of his house, probably praising the God whom his soul loved, when he looked down and saw Bathsheba. He felt a temptation, a thought which tended to sin. The Spirit of God did not fail to convince him of this. He doubtless heard and knew the warning voice, but he yielded in some measure to the thought and the temptation began to prevail over him. His spirit became sullied. He still saw God, but it was more dimly than before. He still loved God, but not in the same degree, not with the same strength and ardor of affection. Yet God checked him again, though His Spirit was grieved and His voice, though fainter and fainter, still whispered, "Sin lieth at the door; look unto me and be saved." But David would not hear. He looked again, not unto God but to the forbidden Bathsheba, till nature became superior to grace and kindled lust in his soul.

The eye of David's mind was now closed again and God vanished out from his sight. Faith—the divine, supernatural interchange with God—and the love of God ceased together. He then rushed on as a horse into battle and knowingly committed the outward sin.

Here is the unquestionable progress from grace to sin. It goes on from step to step. The divine seed of loving, conquering faith remains in him who is born of God. "He keepeth himself" by the grace of God and "cannot commit sin." Then temptation arises. It doesn't matter whether it comes from the world, the flesh, or the devil. The Spirit of God gives warning that sin is near and bids David to watch more in prayer. He gives way, in some degree, to the temptation, which now begins to grow pleasing to him. The Holy Spirit is grieved. His faith is weakened and his love of God grows dim. The Spirit reproves him more sharply and says, "This is the way; walk thou in it." He turns away from the disciplining voice of God and listens to the pleasing voice of the tempter. Evil desire begins and spreads in his soul till faith and love vanish away. He is then capable of committing outward sin, as the power of the Lord has departed from him.

To explain this by another instance, the Apostle Peter was full of faith and of the Holy Spirit, and, keeping faith, he had a conscience void of offense toward God and man. Walking thus in simplicity and godly sincerity, and knowing from God that what God had cleansed was not common or unclean, he ate with the converted Gentiles until the team from Jerusalem arrived. But when they arrived, a temptation arose in his heart "to fear those of the circumcision"—the Jewish converts who were zealous guardians of circumcision and the other Mosaic law rites—and to seek the regard, favor, and praise of these men more than the praise of God.

Peter was warned by the Spirit when sin was near; nevertheless, he yielded to it in some degree. Through sinful fear of man, his faith and love were proportionately weakened.

God reproved him, again, for giving place to the devil. Yet he would not heed the voice of his Shepherd, but gave himself up to slavish fear, thereby quenching the Spirit.

When God disappeared and faith and love became extinct, Peter committed the outward sin, "walking not uprightly," according to the truth of the gospel. He separated himself from his Christian brethren and by his evil example, if not advice also, compelled even the Gentiles to live after the manner of the Jews, entangling themselves again with that yoke of bondage from which Christ had set them free.

Thus it is true that he who is born of God, keeping faith, does not and cannot commit sin. Yet, if he does not keep himself in faith, he may commit all manner of sin with greediness.

From the preceding considerations, we may learn to give a clear and incontestable answer to questions which have frequently perplexed many who were sincere of heart. Does sin precede or follow the loss of faith? Does a child of God first commit sin and thereby lose his faith? Or does he lose his faith first, before he can commit sin?

The more any believer examines his own heart, the more he will be convinced of this, that faith, working by love, excludes both inward and outward sin from any soul watching in prayer. Nevertheless, even then we are liable to temptation, particularly to a sin which easily attacks us. When the loving eye of the soul is steadily fixed on God, the temptation soon vanishes. When it is not and we are drawn out of God by our own desire, caught by the bait of present and promised pleasures, that desire conceived in us brings forth sin. That inward sin having destroyed our faith, we are cast headlong into the snare of the devil, so that we may commit any outward sin.

From this we may learn what the life of God in the soul of a believer is, what it consists of, and what it immediately and necessarily implies. It immediately and necessarily implies the continual inspiration of God's Holy Spirit, God's breathing into the soul and the soul's breathing back what it first receives from God. It is a continual action of God upon the soul, and a reaction of the soul upon God, an unceasing presence of God. It is the loving, pardoning God, manifested to the heart and perceived by faith. It requires an unceasing return of love, praise, and prayer, offering up all the thoughts of our hearts, all the words of our tongues, all the works of our hands, all our body, soul and spirit, to be a holy sacrifice, acceptable to God in Christ Jesus.

From this understanding, we may infer the absolute necessity of this reaction of the soul, whatever it is called, in order to continue the divine life within. *For it plainly appears God does not continue to act upon the soul unless the soul reacts to God.* He presents us with the blessings of His goodness. He first loves us and manifests himself unto us. While we are yet afar off, He calls us to himself and shines upon our hearts. If we do not then love Him who first loved us, if we will not hearken to His voice, if we turn our eyes away from Him and will not attend to the light which He pours in upon us, His Spirit will not always remain in us. He will gradually withdraw and leave us to the darkness of our own hearts. He will not continue to breathe into our souls unless our souls breathe toward Him again, unless our love and prayer and thanksgiving return to Him, a service wherein He is well pleased.

Let us learn, therefore, to follow that direction of the great Apostle Paul, "Be not highminded, but fear." Let us fear sin more than death or hell. Let us have a jealous, though not painful, fear, lest we should listen to our own deceitful hearts. Let him that stands take heed lest he fall. Even he who now stands fast in the grace of God, in the faith that overcomes the world, may nevertheless fall into inward sin and thereby "make shipwreck of his faith." How easily, then, will outward sin regain its dominion over him. We must, therefore, oh men of God, watch always, that we may always hear the voice of God. Watch, that we may pray without ceasing, at all times and in all places, pouring out our hearts before Him. So shall each of us always believe, always love, and never commit sin.

7

*The Difference Between Walking by Sight and Walking by Faith**

We walk by faith, not by sight. (2 Corinthians 5:7)

How short is this description of real Christians, and yet how complete. Here is the sum of the whole experience for those who are truly born of God until the time when they are removed from this life. All true Christian believers are the "we" Paul speaks of. They are not only servants but children of God, and all have the Spirit of adoption, speaking in their hearts Abba, Father. All have the Holy Spirit witnessing with their spirits that they are the sons of God.

These alone can say, "We walk by faith, and not by sight." Before we can possibly walk by faith, we must live by faith and not by sight. All real Christians understand Jesus' words, "Because I live, ye shall live also." We live a life of which the world, whether educated or not, knows

---

*Op. cit., Sermon CXVIII, Vol. 2, pp. 423–428.

nothing. The world is dead in trespass and sin. Through Jesus it is quickened, made alive, given new spiritual senses—senses exercised to discern spiritual good and evil.

To thoroughly understand this important truth, it is necessary to review the whole matter. All the children of men, who are not born of God, walk by sight, having no higher principle. By sight, that is, by bodily senses—sight representing all the senses because it is more extensive than all the rest.

By sight we know of the visible world, from the surface of the earth to the region of the stars. But the world visible to us is only a speck of creation compared to the whole universe or to the invisible world which we cannot see at all. Through the imperfection of our bodily senses, we are left with a great blank.

All our external senses are adapted only to the external, visible world. They are designed to serve us only while we live here, while we dwell in our temporary bodies. The senses have nothing to do with the invisible world and are not adapted to it. They can have no more awareness of the eternal than of the invisible world, although we are as fully assured of the unseen realm as we are of the present world. We cannot think death puts a period to our being. The body indeed turns to dust, but the soul, being of a nobler nature, remains alive. There is an eternal world. How shall we obtain the knowledge of this? What will teach us to draw aside the veil "that hangs 'twixt mortal and immortal being"? We know there is a vast, unbounded prospect before us, but we must say, "Yet the clouds, alas! and darkness rest upon it."

The best of our senses can give us no assistance here nor can our boasted reason. It is now universally allowed, "Nothing is in the understanding which was not first perceived by some of the senses." Consequently, the understanding, having nothing here to work on, can afford us no help at all. In spite of all the information we can gain—either from sense or reason—both the invisible and the eternal world are unknown to all who walk by sight.

Is there no help? Must we remain in total darkness concerning the invisible and the eternal world? We cannot say this. Even the heathen did not all remain in total darkness concerning these two worlds. Some few rays of light have, in all ages and nations, gleamed through the shade. The heavens declare the glory of God, though not to outward sight. The firmament shows the existence of its Maker. From the creation it infers the being of a Creator—powerful and wise, just and merciful. Add to this God, who never, in any age or nation, left himself without a witness in the hearts of men. He gave them rain and fruitful seasons, and thereby imparted some knowledge of Him as the Giver. He is the true light that still, in some degree, enlightens everyone born.

But all these lights put together could only produce a faint twilight. It gave them, even the most enlightened of them, no demonstrative conviction of either the invisible or the eternal world. Some have called Socrates the wisest of all mortal men, that is, of all who were not favored with divine revelation. Yet he had no evidence of another world. Addressing those who had condemned him to death, he said, "And now, oh ye judges, ye are going to live, and I am going to die. Which of these is best, God knows; but I suppose, no man does." What a confession this is. This is all the evidence that poor dying Socrates had, either of an invisible or an eternal world. Even this is preferable to the light of the great and good emperor, Adrian, as he made his pathetic address to his parting soul.

"Poor, little, pretty, fluttering thing,
Must we no longer live together?
And dost thou prune thy trembling wing,
To take thy flight, thou know'st not whither?

> Thy pleasing vein, thy humorous folly,
> Lies all neglected, all forgot!
> And pensive, wavering, melancholy,
> Thou hop'st and fear'st, thou know'st not what."

"Thou know'st not what!" True, there was no knowledge of what was to be hoped or feared after death until Jesus the Righteous arose to dispel all their vain conjectures and brought immortal life to light through the gospel. Then God unveiled and revealed the invisible world. He then revealed himself to the children of men. The Father revealed the Son in their hearts and the Son revealed the Father. He who commanded light to shine out of darkness, shined in their hearts and enlightened them with the knowledge of the glory of God in the face of Jesus Christ.

Faith Opens Our Eyes

Where sense can be of no further use, faith comes to our aid. Faith does what none of the senses can do, even with all the helps that have been invented. All our instruments, however improved by the skill and labor of so many succeeding generations, do not enable us to make any discovery of these unknown regions. They barely serve the occasions for which they were formed in the present visible world.

How different is the case and how vast is the superiority of those who walk by faith. God, having opened the eyes of their understanding, pours divine light into their souls, enabling them to see the invisible—God and the things of God—what their eyes had not seen, nor their ears heard, neither had their hearts conceived.

God, from time to time, reveals all things through the Holy Spirit. When one has entered into the holiest by the blood of Jesus and joined the general assembly and church of the firstborn and God, the Judge of all, and Jesus, the mediator of the new covenant, he can say, "I live not, but Christ lives in me. I now live that life which is with Christ in God. When Christ, who is my life, shall appear, then I shall likewise appear with Him in glory."

They who live by faith, walk by faith. What are the characteristics of those who do this? They regulate all judgments concerning good and evil, not with reference to visible and worldly things, but to things invisible and eternal. They think visible things to be of small value because they pass away like a dream. They consider invisible things to be of high value because they will never pass away. Whatever is invisible is eternal. The things that are not seen do not perish. Paul wrote, "The things which are seen are temporal; but the things which are not seen are eternal. Therefore, they who walk by faith do not desire the things which are seen, neither are they the object of their pursuit. They set their affection on things above, not on things on the earth. They seek only the things that are with Jesus. They know the things that are seen are temporal, passing away like a shadow. Therefore, they do not desire them. They count them as nothing while setting their eyes on things that are not seen and never pass away.

By these they form their judgments of all things. They judge them to be good or evil, promoting or hindering their spiritual welfare, for eternity. They weigh whatever occurs in this balance, "What influence has this on my eternal state?" They regulate all their tempers and passions, all their desires, joys and fears, by this standard. They regulate all their thoughts and designs, all their words and actions, to prepare them for that invisible world to which they are soon going. They do not dwell but only sojourn here, not looking upon earth as their home. They are only passing through it to a higher world.

Are you of this group, who are now here before God? Do you see Him who is invisible? Have you faith, living faith, the faith of a child? Can you say, "The life which I now live . . . I live by the faith of the Son of God, who loved me, and gave himself for me"? Do you walk by faith? Hear the question! I do not ask whether you curse or swear or profane the Sabbath or live in any outward sin. I do not ask whether you do good or attend all the ordinances of church. Even if you are blameless in all these respects, I ask, in the name of God, by what standard do you judge the value of things? Is it by the visible or by the invisible world?

Make this matter an issue at once! Which do you judge best, that your son should be a pious worker or a profane leader? Which appears better to you, that your daughter should be a child of God and walk on foot or a child of the devil and travel in style? When the question concerns the marriage of your daughter, think carefully whether you consider her body more than her soul. Know yourself. You are on the way to hell and not to heaven if you walk by sight and not by faith. I do not ask whether you live in any outward sin or neglect, but whether you generally seek the things that are above or the things that are here. Do you set your affection on things of heaven or things of earth? If on the latter, you are as much on the path of destruction as a thief or drunkard. Let everyone among you deal honestly with themselves. Ask your own heart, *what am I seeking* day by day? What do I desire? Am I pursuing earth or heaven, things seen or things unseen? What is your object, God or the world? As the Lord lives, if the world is your object, all your religion is vain.

See to it, from now on at least, you choose the better part. Let your judgment of all the things around you be according to their real value, with reference to the invisible and eternal world. See that you judge everything according to the influence it will have on your eternal state. Let your affection, your desire, your joy, your hope, be set not on transient objects, not on things that fly like shadows or pass away like dreams. Set them on things that are incapable of change, that are incorruptible and never fade away. Let all you think, speak, and do be fixed on Him who is invisible and the glories that shall be revealed. Then your whole body will be full of light, your whole soul will enjoy the light of God's countenance, and you will continually see the light of the glorious love of God in the face of Jesus.

In particular, let all your desire be to Him and to the remembrance of His name. Beware of foolish and harmful desires which might arise from any visible or temporal thing. John warns us against the love of the world. It is not so much to the faithless as it is to the faithful that he warns, "Love not the world, neither the things that are in the world."

Avoid the desires of the flesh, the gratification of the outward senses. Shun the desire of the eye, the internal senses, the imagination. Give no place to the pride of life, the desire for wealth, pomp, or honor that comes from men. John confirms this advice by an observation paralleling Paul's to the Corinthians: "The fashion of this world passeth away." The fashion of it—all worldly objects, business, pleasures, cares, whatever now attracts our attention—passes away. By the very act of passing, it will not return. Therefore, desire none of these fleeting things, but only that glory which abides forever.

Observe well, this alone is true Christian religion, not any other opinion or system of opinions, however true, however scriptural. These are commonly called faith, but those who believe opinions to be true Christianity are given up to a strong delusion. If they suppose easy doctrines to be a sure passport to heaven, they are on the high road to hell. Christianity is not harmlessness. Believing it sends thousands to the bottomless pit. Christianity is not morality, important as morality is. Morality not built on a foundation of loving faith is of no value in God's sight. Christianity is not the most formal, exact observance of all the ordinances of God. That too, unless built on the right foundation, is no more pleasing to God than those who "have chosen their own ways, and their soul delighteth in their abominations."

Christianity is no less than living in eternity and walking in eternity. By this, one is walking in the love of God and man, in lowliness, meekness, and resignation. This, and this alone, is that life which is hidden with Christ in God. Only one who experiences this dwells in God and God in him. This alone is setting the crown on Christ's head and doing His will on earth as it is done in heaven.

It is easily seen that this is the very thing men of the world call fanaticism, a word fit for their purpose since no one can tell its meaning. If it has any sense at all, it means a sort of religious madness. When you give your witness, they immediately cry out, "Too much religion has made you mad." All that you experience, either of the invisible or of the eternal world, they call only the wild dreams of a heated imagination. It cannot be otherwise, when men born blind believe themselves experts on color and light. They will readily call anyone insane who declares the existence of things they cannot conceive.

From all that has been said, the nature of that fashionable thing called dissipation may be seen clearly. It is the very quintessence of agnosticism and atheism. That is the art of forgetting God and being completely without God in the world. It is the art of excluding Him, if not out of the world He has created, at least out of the minds of all His intelligent creatures. It is a total studied inattention to the whole invisible and eternal world, especially to death, the gate of eternity, and to those important consequences of death—heaven and hell.

This is the real nature of dissipation. It is not a harmless thing. It is one of the choicest instruments for the destruction of our immortal spirits ever forged in the armory of hell. It has been the means of plunging myriads of souls, who might have enjoyed the glory of God, into the everlasting fire prepared for the devil and his angels. It blots out all Christianity in one stroke and levels man to the beasts that perish. All you who fear God, flee from dissipation. Dread and abhor it.

Strive to have God in all your thoughts, to have eternity ever in your eye. Look continually, not at things that are seen, but at the things which are not seen. Let your hearts be fixed where Christ sits at the right hand of God. Then, when He calls you, "An entrance may be ministered unto you abundantly into His everlasting kingdom."

8

*On the Discoveries of Faith**

Now faith is . . . the evidence of things not seen. (Hebrews 11:1).

For many ages intelligent men have known there is nothing in the understanding which was not first perceived by some of our bodily senses. All the knowledge which we naturally have comes originally from our senses. Therefore, those who lack a sense cannot have the least knowledge or idea of the objects of that sense. Those who have never had sight have no knowledge or conception of light or color. Indeed, some have tried to prove that we have innate ideas, not derived from any of the senses but coexisting with our understanding. It is agreed by all impartial persons that although some things are so plain and obvious we can hardly avoid knowing them; once we use our understanding, the knowledge even of these is not innate but derived from some of our senses.

There is a great difference between our senses. They are avenues of knowledge, but some have a very limited sphere of action and some a more extensive one. By feel-

---

Op. cit., Sermon CXV, Vol. 2, pp. 406–410.

ing, we can discern only those objects that touch some part of our body, and, consequently, this sense extends only to a small number of objects. Our senses of taste and smell extend to fewer still. On the other hand, our nobler sense of hearing has a very wide sphere of action, especially in the case of loud sounds, such as thunder, the roaring of the sea, or the firing of a cannon. The latter has been heard at distances of many miles. Yet the space to which the sense of hearing itself extends is small compared to that of the sense of sight.

Sight takes in, at one view, not only the most unbounded prospects on earth, but also the moon, planets, the sun and stars. Despite all this, not even sight can reach beyond the bounds of the visible world.

All our senses supply us with enough knowledge of the material world to accomplish the purposes of life. Beyond this they cannot go. They furnish us with no information at all about the invisible world.

Our Eyes of Faith

Our wise and gracious Governor of the worlds, both visible and invisible, has prepared a remedy for this defect. God has appointed faith to supply the defect of sense, to take us up where sense lets us down, and to help us over the great gulf. It begins where sense ends. Sense is an evidence of things that are seen—of the visible, the material world, and the several parts of it. Faith, on the other hand, is the evidence of things not seen—of the invisible world, of all those invisible things which are revealed in the Scriptures. But Scriptures reveal nothing and are a mere dead letter if they are not mixed with faith in those who study them.

In particular, faith is an evidence to me of the existence of that unseen thing, my own soul. Without faith I would be in utter uncertainty concerning my soul. By faith I know my soul is an immortal spirit made in the image of God. In His natural and moral image it has an incorruptible picture of the God of glory. By that same evidence I know I have fallen short of the glorious image of God. I know we are all dead in trespasses and sins, so utterly dead that nothing good dwells in us, and we are inclined to all evil, totally unable to bring our own souls alive.

By faith I know that, besides the souls of men, there are other kinds of spirits. I believe that millions of creatures walk the earth, unseen. These I call angels, and I believe part of them are holy and happy and the other part wicked and miserable. I believe the good angels are sent by God to continually minister to the heirs of salvation, who ultimately will be equal to angels, although they are now inferior to them. I believe the latter, the evil angels called devils or demons in Scripture, are united under one head, Satan, who is the chief adversary of both God and man. He and his slaves, called the princes of the power of the air, either roam the upper regions or walk about the earth as roaring lions, seeking whom they may devour.

I know by faith that above all these is the Lord God, who is, who was, and who is to come. He is God everlasting, without end. He fills heaven and earth. He is infinite in power, in justice, in mercy and in holiness. He has created all things, visible and invisible, by the breath of His mouth. He still upholds them all and preserves them in being by the word of His power. He governs all things that are in heaven above, in earth beneath, and under the earth. By faith I know there are three who bear record in heaven—the Father, the Son, and the Holy Spirit—and that these three are one. The Word is God the Son, who was made flesh, lived and died for our salvation, rose again, ascended into heaven and now sits at the right hand of the Father.

By faith I know the Holy Spirit is the giver of all spiritual life, of righteousness, peace, and joy in the Holy

Spirit, of holiness and happiness, by the restoration of that image of God in which we are created. Of all these things, faith is the evidence—the sole evidence—to the children of men.

As the information which we receive from our senses does not extend to the invisible world, neither does it extend to the eternal world. In spite of all the instruction which either sight or any of the senses can give, they do not let in one ray of light to discover the secrets of the limitless eternity. This, the eternal world, begins at death, the death of every individual person. The moment the breath of man leaves him, he is an inhabitant of eternity. Just then, time vanishes away as a dream when one awakens.

Here, again, faith takes the place of sense and gives us a view of things to come. It draws aside the veil which hangs between mortal and immortal beings. Faith reveals to us the souls of the righteous, immediately received by the holy angels, and carried by those ministering spirits into Abraham's bosom, into the delights of paradise, the garden of God where the light of His countenance perpetually shines. This is where the soul converses, not only with his former relations, friends and fellow soldiers, but with the saints of all nations and all ages, with the glorious dead of ancient days, with the noble army of martyrs, the apostles, the prophets, the patriarchs, Abraham, Isaac and Jacob. Above all this, he will be with Jesus in a manner that he could not be while he remained in the body.

Faith also reveals the unholy and evil angels. They torment here before the end of the world, when everyone will receive judgment, recompense or reward. Until then, they are employed by Satan in advancing his infernal kingdom and doing all the mischief that lies in their power to the poor, weak children of men. They carry their own hell with them, in diabolical, infernal tempers, giving a consciousness of guilt and of the wrath of God, which continually gnaws at human spirits. This essential misery they cannot shake off, any more than they can shake off their own being, except by faith.

Faith opens another scene in the eternal world. We can see the coming of our Lord in the clouds of heaven to judge both the quick and the dead. It enables us to see the great white throne coming down from heaven and the Lord who sits on the throne, from whose face the heavens and the earth flee. We see the dead, small and great, standing before God. We see the books opened, and the dead judged according to the things that are written in the books. We see the earth and the sea giving up their dead, and hell giving up its dead for the final judgment that must come to everyone according to his own works.

By faith we are also shown the immediate consequences of the general judgment. We see the execution of that happy sentence pronounced upon those on the right hand, "Come, ye blessed of my Father, inherit the kingdom prepared for you from the foundation of the world." After which, the holy angels tune their harps and sing, "Lift up your heads, oh ye gates, and be ye lifted up, ye everlasting doors, that the heirs of glory may come in!" Then we shall drink of the rivers of pleasure that are at God's right hand for everyone.

We see, also, the execution of that dreadful sentence pronounced on those on the left hand, "Depart from me, ye cursed, into everlasting fire, prepared for the devil and his angels." Then shall the ministers of divine vengeance plunge them into the lake of fire burning with brimstone, where they have no rest day or night, but the smoke of their torment ascends forever and ever.

In addition to the invisible and the eternal world, which are not seen and which are discoverable only by faith, there is a whole system of things which are not seen, which cannot be discerned by any of our outward senses. I mean the spiritual world which is the kingdom of God in the soul of man. Eye has not seen, nor ear heard, neither can it enter into the heart of man to conceive the things of this interior kingdom unless God has revealed it by His Spirit. The Holy Spirit prepares us for His inward kingdom by removing the veil from our heart and enabling us to know ourselves as we are known by Him. The Spirit convinces us of sin, of our evil nature, our evil tempers, and our evil words and actions, and we are compelled to plead guilty before God. At the same time, we receive the fear of the wrath of God, the fear of punishment we have deserved, and, above all, fear of death that it might consign us over to eternal death. Souls who are thus convinced feel themselves imprisoned, completely sinful, completely guilty and completely helpless. This conviction implies a kind of faith. It is the evidence of things not seen or possible to be seen or known until God reveals them to us.

The Importance of a Growing Faith

An important point is that this faith is only the faith of a servant and not the faith of a son. This is a point which many do not clearly understand. The faith of a servant implies a divine evidence of the invisible and the external world. It is the evidence of the spiritual world so far as it can exist without living experience. Whoever has attained the faith of a servant fears God and avoids evil. Peter called it fearing God and working righteousness, and, consequently, being accepted by God to a degree.

Elsewhere, the servant is described in these words, "he that feareth God, and keepeth His commandments." One who has gone thus far in religion, who obeys God out of fear, is not in any way to be scorned, because the fear of the Lord is the beginning of wisdom. Nevertheless, the servant should be encouraged not to stop there, not to rest until he attains the adoption of a son, until he obeys Him out of love which is the privilege of all the children of God. Exhort him to press on by all possible means, until he passes from faith to faith, from the faith of a servant to the faith of a son, from the spirit of fearful bondage to the spirit of childlike love, with Christ revealed in his heart. He can then testify, "The life which I now live in the flesh I live by the faith of the Son of God, who loved me, and gave himself for me."

He will then be born of God, inwardly changed by the mighty power of God from an earthly, sensual, devilish mind, to the mind which was in Christ Jesus. He will experience what Paul means by his remarkable words to the Galatians, "Because ye are sons, God hath sent forth the Spirit of his Son into your hearts, crying Abba, Father." John observed that he who believes as a son has the witness in himself. The Spirit himself witnesses with his spirit that he is a child of God. The love of God is shed abroad in his heart by the Holy Spirit which is given to him.

Many doubts and fears may still remain, even in a child of God, while he is weak in faith, while he is among the number of those whom Paul termed "babes in Christ." When his faith is strengthened, when he receives faith's abiding impression of things to come, when he receives the abiding witness of the Spirit, doubts and fears vanish. Then he enjoys the full assurance of faith without any doubt or fear.

To those whom he calls young men, John says, "I have written unto you, young men, because ye are strong, and the word of God abideth in you, and ye have overcome the wicked one." By this John means the pardoning word, the word which forgave all their sins. In consequence of their forgiveness they know they have unceasing divine favor.

To these, especially, we direct Paul's exhortation to leave the first principles of the doctrine of Christ, repentance and faith, and go on to perfection. In what sense are we to leave those principles? Only by not fixing our whole attention on them and thinking and talking of nothing else, as we are to retain both one and the other, the knowledge of ourselves and the knowledge of God, to our lives' end. But we are to seek perfection.

What is the perfection Paul tells us to seek? It is not only a deliverance from doubts and fears but from sin, from all inward and outward sin, from evil desires, and evil tempers, as well as from evil words and works. It is not only a deliverance from all evil dispositions implied in the expression, "The Lord thy God will circumcise thine heart," but the planting of all good dispositions in their place. This is what is meant by the expression, "to love the Lord thy God with all thine heart, and with all your soul."

These are the ones to whom John gives the venerable title of fathers, those who have known the eternal three-in-one God from the beginning. One of them expressed it as bearing about himself an air of truth taught by experience and a fullness of the ever blessed Trinity. Those who are fathers in Christ generally enjoy the full assurance of hope. They have no more doubt of reigning with Him in glory than if they already saw Him coming in the clouds of heaven, but this does not prevent their continually increasing in the knowledge and love of God. While they rejoice evermore and pray without ceasing, they give thanks in everything. They pray that they may never cease to watch, to deny themselves, to take up their cross daily, to fight the good fight of faith against the world, the devil and their own manifold infirmities. They pray to be able to comprehend with all saints what is the length and breadth and height and depth and to know that immeasurable love of Jesus Christ which surpasses all knowledge. They pray to be filled with all the fullness of God.

9

*An Israelite Indeed**

Behold an Israelite indeed, in whom is no guile. (John 1:47)

Some years ago, two very ingenious arguments were published on the origin of our ideas of beauty and virtue. In one it was maintained that the very essence of virtue is the love of our fellow creatures. It endeavored to prove that virtue and benevolence are one and the same thing, and that every temper is only virtuous as it partakes of the nature of benevolence. All our words and actions are only virtuous, then, when they spring from that principle. Did the writer think gratitude, or the love of God, is the foundation of this benevolence? Quite the contrary, such a thought never entered his mind. He maintained that any thought or action produced by a regard for God or for seeking a reward from Him is not virtuous at all, and the more there is of the view to God, the less there is of virtue.

That essay is a dangerous attack on the whole of the Christian revelation, which asserts the love of God to be

---

*Op. cit., Sermon XCV, Vol. 2, pp. 274–278.

the true foundation, both of the love of our neighbor and of all other virtues. Christianity places it as the first and great commandment on which all the rest depend, "Thou shalt love the Lord thy God with all thy heart, and with all thy soul, and with all thy mind, and with all thy strength." According to the Bible, benevolence, or the love of our neighbor, is only the second commandment. If Scripture is of God, benevolence alone cannot be both the foundation and the essence of all virtue. Benevolence itself has no virtue at all, unless it springs from the love of God.

The essay has a marginal note in favor of Christianity. "Who would not wish," it says, "that the Christian revelation could be proved to be of God, seeing it is unquestionably the most benevolent institution that ever appeared in the world?" This statement, if considered carefully, is yet another blow at the very root of that revelation. It is actually saying, "I wish it could, but, in truth, it cannot be proved."

Still another ingenious writer advances a totally different hypothesis, endeavoring to prove that truth is the essence of virtue. This one goes further from the Bible than the earlier writer, who only set aside one of the two great commandments, namely, "Thou shalt love the Lord thy God." This man sets aside both, for his hypothesis does not place the essence of virtue in either the love of God or of our neighbor.

Both of these authors agree, though in different ways, to pull apart what God has joined. Paul unites them together in teaching us to speak the truth in love. In the scripture, truth and love were united in one by Him who knows the hearts of all men, when He says of Nathanael, "Behold an Israelite indeed, in whom is no guile."

Who is this Nathanael, who receives such a glorious testimony from Jesus? Isn't it strange that he is not mentioned again in any part of the New Testament? He is not mentioned again under this name, but he probably had another more common name. Early scholars believed he was Bartholemew, one of our Lord's apostles. Both Matthew and Mark list him immediately after Philip, who first brought him to the Master. It is very probable that his proper name was Nathanael, a name common among the Jews, and that his other name, Bartholomew, meaning son of Ptolemy, was taken from his father. At that time this was common practice among both the Jews and the heathen.

By what little is said of him, he appears to have been a man of an excellent spirit, not quick to believe yet open to conviction and willing to receive the truth. So we read that Philip found Nathanael, probably by accident, and told him they had found Jesus of Nazareth, of whom Moses and the prophets wrote. It was Nathanael who asked, "Can any good thing come out of Nazareth?"

Philip told him to come and see and judge for himself. Nathanael took this advice without having to confer with anyone. When Jesus saw him coming and pronounced him without guile, "Nathanael saith unto Him, Whence knowest Thou me? Jesus answered and said unto him, Before that Philip called thee, when thou wast under the fig tree, I saw thee." Nathanael then declared, "Rabbi, Thou art the Son of God! Thou art the King of Israel!"

The Truthful Heart

What is implied in our Lord's words, "In whom is no guile"? It may include all that is contained in the advice, "Still let thy heart be true to God, thy words to it, thy actions to them both."

Having our hearts true implies no less than is included in God's gracious command, "My son, give me thy heart." *Our heart is only true to God when we give it to Him.* We give Him our heart in the lowest degree when we seek our happiness in Him, when we neither seek it in gratifying the desire of the flesh in any of the sensual pleasures nor in gratifying the desire of the eye in any of the pleasures of the imagination.

Seeking our happiness in God is not finding it in the pride of life, in the honor that comes to men in being loved, esteemed, and applauded, neither in pleasure in new or beautiful objects, whether of nature or art, nor in "laying up treasures on earth." When we seek happiness in none of these, but only in God, then we, in some sense, give Him our heart.

In a greater sense we give God our heart when we not only seek but find happiness in Him. This happiness starts when we first know Him by the teaching of His own Spirit, when it pleases the Father to reveal His Son in our hearts, so we can humbly say, "My Lord and my God." Also when the Son is pleased to reveal His Father in us by the Spirit of adoption crying in our hearts, "Abba, Father," and bearing His testimony to our spirits that we are the children of God. Then it is that God sheds His love in our hearts. *According to the degree of our love is the degree of our happiness.*

I have been asked whether it is God's plan that the happiness, which is at first enjoyed by all who know and love Him, should continue any longer than the day it is received. In many it does not. In a few months, perhaps weeks or even days, the joy and peace either vanishes at once or gradually. If God is willing for their happiness to continue, how can this be explained?

Jude's exhortation, "Keep yourselves in the love of God," certainly implies that something is to be done on our part in order for it to continue. This agrees with the declaration of our Lord, concerning this and every gift of God, "Unto everyone that hath shall be given, and he shall have abundance: but from him that hath not [does not use or improve it] shall be taken away even that which he hath." Therefore, whoever improves the grace he has already received, whoever increases in the love of God, will surely retain it. God will continue, yes, will give it even more abundantly. Whoever does not improve this talent cannot possibly retain it. If he does not, it will be taken away from him.

The Truthful Tongue

Meantime, as the heart of him who is "an Israelite indeed," is true to God, his words are also. As there is no guile lodged in his heart, so is none found on his lips. The first thing implied here is veracity, speaking the truth from his heart, putting away all willful lying of every kind and degree. A lie, according to a well-known definition of it, is "a falsehood known to be such by the speaker, uttered with an intention to deceive." But even the speaking of a falsehood is not a lie if it is not spoken with an intent to deceive.

Most lies can be divided into three types. The first type is malicious, the second is harmless, and the third is officious. No one excuses or defends malicious lies. Such are told with a design to hurt someone and are condemned by all. Judgment is more divided in regard to harmless lies, supposed to do neither good nor harm. Many, even in the Christian world, utter them without any scruple and maintain that if they do no harm to anyone else, they do none to the speaker. Whether they do or not, they certainly have no place in the mouth of one who is "an Israelite indeed." He cannot tell lies in jest any more than in earnest. Nothing but truth is heard from his mouth. He remembers the express command of God to the Ephesian

Christians: "Putting away all lying, speak every man truth with his neighbor."

There have been numerous controversies in the Christian church over officious lies, those spoken with a design to do good. Many writers and other men renowned for piety and learning have published volumes on the subject, not only maintaining them to be innocent but commending them as meritorious. But what does the Bible say? One passage is so clear we need no other. It occurs in Romans 3:7: "If the truth of God hath more abounded through my lie unto glory, why yet am I also judged as a sinner?" Won't the good effect of a lie excuse it from blame?

Paul plainly declares that a good result from a lie is no excuse for it and a slander on Christians to accuse them of teaching men to do evil so good may come. Anyone teaching men to do evil so good may result, or doing so themselves, is justly damned. This is particularly applicable to those who tell lies in order to bring good. Therefore, officious lies, as well as all others, are an abomination to the God of truth. God's requirement, however strange it may sound, is in the ancient saying, "I would not tell a willful lie to save the souls of the whole world."

The second thing implied in the character of "an Israelite indeed" is sincerity. As veracity is opposed to lying, so sincerity is opposed to cunning, but is consistent with wisdom or discretion. Wisdom and cunning are entirely different. Wisdom is the faculty of discerning the best ends and the most suitable means of attaining them. True prudence, in the general sense of the word, is the same as wisdom. Discretion is simply another name for prudence, sometimes referring to our outward behavior and meaning right words and actions. Cunning, on the other hand, is no better and no worse than the art of deceiving. If, therefore, it contains any wisdom at all, it is the wisdom from below, springing from the bottomless pit and leading down to the place from which it came.

The two great means which cunning uses in order to deceive are simulation and dissimulation. Simulation is seeming to be what we are not. Dissimulation is seeming not to be what we are. Both are commonly called flying under false colors. Simulation puts on innumerable faces in order to deceive. Dissimulation uses almost as many for the same purpose. But the sincere Christian shuns them and always appears exactly what he is.

Suppose we are engaged with crafty men. If they ask tricky questions, is it acceptable to use silence without being judged cunning? Not only may we, we ought, on many occasions, to be completely silent or speak with as much reserve as circumstances require. To say nothing at all, in many cases, is consistent with the highest sincerity. It is the same to speak with reserve, to say only a part of what we know. However, to pretend that part to be the whole would be contrary to sincerity.

A more difficult consideration is whether we may speak the truth in order to deceive. Like the man of old who broke out into an exclamation of applause for his own ingenuity, "This I take to be my masterpiece, to deceive them both by speaking the truth." May we do the same? A heathen might pride himself on this, but not a Christian. Although it is not contrary to veracity, it certainly is to sincerity. The proper course to follow, if we judge it necessary to speak at all, is to avoid both simulation and dissimulation and to speak the naked truth, straight from the heart.

This may be termed simplicity, but it goes a little further than sincerity itself. It implies not only speaking no known falsehood but also making sure to deceive no one. We should speak plainly and simply to everyone when we speak at all, speaking as little children, in a childlike but

not childish manner. We must totally refrain from using
flattery. I quite agree with the poet, "It never was a good
day, since lowly fawning was called compliment." I advise
Christians of sincerity and simplicity never to allow flattery out of their mouths.

The Bishop of Rochester was once asked, "Why will
you not let your servants spare you, when you do not care
to see company? Let them say you are not at home. That
deceives no one, for everyone knows it means only that
you are busy."

He replied, "I am sure it is not consistent with that
simplicity which becomes a Christian bishop."

The sincerity and simplicity of one in whom there is
no guile will influence the person's entire behavior. These
color the whole conversation, which is plain and artless
and free from all disguise, and the very picture of a pure
heart. The truth and love which reign there produce an
open front and a serene countenance. He opens a window
in his breast for all the world to see no pretense lingers
there.

This, then, is real, genuine, solid virtue—not truth
alone nor conformity to truth. This is a property of real
virtue, not the essence of it. Not love alone, though this
comes nearer the mark. Love, in one sense, is the fulfilling
of the law, but truth and love united are the essence of
virtue or holiness. God indispensably requires inward
truth to influence all our words and actions. Yet truth,
itself, separate from love, is nothing in His sight. The
humble, gentle, patient love of all mankind must be fixed
on its right foundation, namely the love of God springing
from faith, from a full conviction that God has given His
only Son to die for *my* sins. Then the whole world will
resolve into that grand conclusion, worthy of all men to
be received, "Neither circumcision availeth any thing, nor
uncircumcision, but faith that worketh by love."

10

*Causes of the Inefficacy of Christianity**

Is there no balm in Gilead; is there no physician there? Why then is not the health of the daughter of my people recovered? (Jeremiah 8:22)

This question of Jeremiah's relates only to the people of Israel. Let us think of it in a general sense, in relation to all mankind. Then let us inquire why Christianity has done so little good in the world. Is not Christianity the balm, the outward means, which the great Physician has given for the restoration of spiritual health?

It was intended by our all wise and almighty Creator to be a remedy for that corruption, a universal remedy for a universal evil. Unfortunately, it has not answered this intention. It never did and it does not today. The disease still remains in full strength. Wickedness of every kind, in all its forms, still covers the face of the earth. Why, then, is that health not restored? Here is the problem.

O Lord God, You are righteous. Still we plead with You,

Op. cit., Sermon CXX, Vol. 2, pp. 435–440.

asking about this. Have You forgotten the world You made, which You created for Your glory? Can You despise the work of Your own hands, the purchase of Your Son's blood? You have given medicine to heal our sickness, yet our sickness is not healed. Darkness still covers the earth and Your people, "Darkness such as devils feel, issuing from the pit of hell."

What a mystery this is, why Christianity has done so little good in the world. Can any account be given or any reasons assigned? There are still many inhabitants of the earth who know little of it, so it is no wonder they draw no advantage from Christianity.

Why is it that little advantage is derived from it by the Christian world? Are Christians better than other men, better than the irreligious? If the truth were told, some Christians appear to be worse. In many respects they are much worse, but many of these are not truly Christians. The majority of those who call themselves Christians do not know what Christianity is. They do not understand it any better than they do Greek or Hebrew; therefore, they cannot be better for it. What do the so-called Christians of various churches know? Have they any conception of worshiping God in spirit and in truth? How exceedingly little they know, either of outward or inward Christianity. How many thousands, calling themselves Christians, know nothing more of Christianity than the name. They know little more than pagans.

Christianity is well known to all the inhabitants of the Western world, a great part of which is termed Christendom, the land of Christians. Part of these are still members of the church of Rome and part are called Protestants. As to the former—the Portuguese, Spaniards, Italians, French, and Germans—what do the bulk of them know of scriptural Christianity? Having had frequent opportunity of conversing with many of these, both at home and abroad, I can boldly affirm that they are in general totally ignorant of the theory and practice of Christianity. They are perishing by the thousands for lack of knowledge, knowing little of the very first principles of Christianity.

I wish this were not altogether the case of the Protestants of Europe. I believe there are many knowing Christians among them, but I doubt that one in ten, or even one in fifty, know His Spirit. Certainly not, if we judge by those we find in Great Britain and Ireland. Do the people of England, in general, understand Christianity? Do they conceive what it is? Can they give an intelligible account of either the speculative or practical part of it? Do they know the very first principles of the natural and moral attributes of God? Do they understand the redemption of man, the offices of Christ, the operations of the Holy Spirit? Do they know anything of justification, of the new birth, of outward and inward sanctification?

Mention any of these things to the next ten persons you meet and you will find nine out of the ten are ignorant of all these parts of Christianity. Most of the inhabitants of the Scotch Highlands are just as ignorant concerning these as are the Protestants in Ireland. Make a fair inquiry, not only in the country but in the cities, to discover how few know what Christianity means. The number you will find that have any conception of the analogy of faith, of the connected chain of Scripture truths, and their relation to each other—the natural corruption of man, justification by faith, the new birth, and inward and outward holiness—is small. Anyone who is observant sees that a vast majority know no more of Christianity than of Judaism or Islam. What good can Christianity do for these who are ignorant of it?

In some parts of the Western world, however, scriptural Christianity is well known. In the large cities and towns, Christianity is openly and widely declared. Thousands upon thousands continually hear and receive the truth that is in Jesus. Why is it, then, that even in these parts Christianity has had so little effect? Why are the "Christian" people here generally no better than the irreligious?

A common saying among the Christians in the early church was, "The soul and the body make a man, the spirit and discipline make a Christian." This implies that none could be real Christians without the help of Christian discipline. If this is so, it is small wonder we find so few Christians. Where is Christian discipline? In what part of Christendom is Christian discipline added to Christian doctrine? Whatever doctrine is preached, without discipline it cannot have its full effect on its hearers.

To narrow it down still more, scriptural Christianity is preached and generally known among the people commonly called "Methodists." They have Christian discipline and it is constantly exercised in all the essential branches. Why, then, are these who have both doctrine and discipline not complete Christians? Why is the spiritual health of the Methodists incomplete? Why do they not have in them the mind that was also in Christ Jesus? Why have we not learned His very first lesson, to be meek and lowly of heart, to say with Him in all circumstances of life, "Not as I will, but as Thou wilt!" "I have come not to do my own will, but the will of him who sent me."

A Grip Too Tight to Give

Why are we not crucified to the world, and the world to us? Why don't all of us live the life that is hid with Christ in God? Why do we not walk as Christ also walked? He has left us examples that we might tread in his steps, but we pay no attention to them. Few hear the solemn words, "Lay not up for yourself treasures upon earth." Of the three rules given to me for a sermon on the mammon of unrighteousness, you may find many who observe the first rule, "Earn all you can." A few may observe the second, "Save all you can." But not many can be found who observe the third rule, "Give all you can." There is no reason to believe that even five hundred can be found among fifty thousand so-called Methodists, who give all they can. Yet nothing can be more plain than the fact that all who observe only the first two rules, without the third, will be two times more the children of hell than they ever were before.

Oh that God would enable me once more, before I leave this earth, to lift my voice like a trumpet to all those who earn and save all they can, but do not give all they can. They are the ones, some of them most highly placed ones, who continually grieve the Holy Spirit of God and in a great measure stop His gracious influence from descending on our assemblies. Many of our brethren, beloved of God, have no food to eat, no clothes to wear, and no place to lay their heads. They are in this sad state because you impiously, unjustly, and cruelly keep from them what your Lord and Master, and theirs, places in your hands for the purpose of supplying their wants.

There are many poor members of Christ, pinched with hunger, shivering with cold, half naked, while others have plenty of this world's goods for food, drink, and apparel. In the name of God, what are we doing? Do you neither fear God nor regard man? Why do you not give your bread to the hungry and cover the naked with some clothes? Have you spent on your own costly apparel money that could have gone to these more worthy causes? Did God command you do this? Does he commend you for it? Did He entrust you with His, not your, goods for this purpose, and does He now say, "Servant of God, well done"? You well know He does not. Such idle expense gains no approval, either from God or from your own conscience. If you argue you can afford it, you should be ashamed to utter such miserable nonsense. Don't utter such whining stupidity, such palpable absurdity. No steward can afford to be an arrogant rogue, wasting his master's goods. No servant can afford to spend his master's money in any way other than he has been instructed. Whoever does this ought to be excluded from a Christian society.

Is it possible to supply all the poor in our society with the necessities of life? It was possible once to do this in a larger society than this. In the first church at Jerusalem there was no one among them who needed anything because distribution was made among them according to need. There are examples of this, today, among the Quakers and among the United Brethren (the so-called Moravians). Why should we not be able to do the same? If they are ten times richer than we, or even fifty times, it should make no difference, as long as we are equally willing.

A Methodist told me several years ago, "I shall leave forty thousand pounds to my children." Suppose he had left them just twenty thousand and given the other twenty thousand to God and the poor. Would God have called him a fool? This one act would have lifted his entire congregation far from want.

I will not talk of giving, or leaving, half of your fortune to God, as you might think this too high a price even for heaven. I will give you lower terms. Surely there are some among you who could give a hundred pounds, perhaps some who could give a thousand, and still leave your children enough. With two thousand pounds we could supply the present needs of all our poor and set them up to supply their own needs for the future. Now suppose this could be done, are we clear before God while it is not done? The neglect of this is one reason why so many among us are still sick and weak, both in soul and body. We grieve the Holy Spirit by preferring the customs of the world to the commands of God.

I often wonder if we preachers are not in some measure partakers of the sin of those who refuse to give freely. I wonder whether it is not a kind of partiality, perhaps a great sin, to keep them in our churches. I wonder if we aren't hurting their souls by encouraging them to persevere in walking contrary to the Bible. Would this not, in some measure, intercept the salutary influences of the blessed Spirit on the whole community?

Indulgence Rather Than Denial

Simply put, Christianity has had such a small impact because the Church has forgotten, or at least not duly attended to, those solemn words of our Lord, "If any man will come after me, let him deny himself, and take up his cross, and follow me." Several years ago a holy man remarked, "Never was there before a people in the Christian church who had so much of the power of God among them, with so little self-denial." Indeed the work of God does go on, and in a surprising manner, notwithstanding this capital defect. But it cannot go on in the same degree as it otherwise would, and the Word of God cannot have its full effect unless the hearers of the Word deny themselves and take up their crosses daily.

It would be easy to show how the Methodists, in general, are deplorably wanting in the practice of Christian self-denial, from which they have been continually frightened by the silly outcries of the Antinomians. While we were at Oxford, the rule of every Methodist was, unless we were ill, to fast every Wednesday and Friday, in imitation of the early church, for which we had the highest reverence. This practice of the early church is universally known. "Who does not know," says Epiphanius, an ancient writer, "that the fasts of the fourth and sixth days of the week are observed by the Christians throughout the whole world?" For several years all the Methodists, without any exception, did this until some in London carried it to excess and fasted to the point of impairment of health. It was not long before others made this a pretext for not fasting at all. I fear there are now thousands of Methodists, both in England and Ireland, who are following the same bad example. They not only don't fast twice a week, they don't even fast twice a month. And are there not some of you who do not fast one single day from the beginning of the year to the end? What excuse can there be for this? According to Scripture, the person who never fasts is no more on the way to heaven than the person who never prays.

Why is self-denial practiced so little? Why is so very little of it to be found even in the oldest and largest congregations? The more I observe and consider things, the more clearly I see the cause of this. We grow more and more self-indulgent because we grow rich. Although many of us are still deplorably poor, many others, in the space of twenty, thirty, or forty years, are twenty, thirty, or forty times richer than they were when they first entered the church. This is an observation which admits of few exceptions. Nine out of ten of these congregations decreased in grace in the same porportion as they increased in wealth. Indeed, according to the natural tendency of riches, we cannot expect it to be otherwise.

This is an astonishing thing. How can we understand it? It seems that Christianity, true scriptural Christianity, has a tendency, in the process of time, to undermine and destroy itself. For wherever true Christianity spreads, it must cause diligence and frugality, which, in the natural course of things must beget riches. Riches naturally beget pride, love of the world, and every temper that is destructive to Christianity. Now, if there is no way to prevent this, Christianity is inconsistent with itself and of consequence cannot stand, cannot continue long among any people, since wherever it generally prevails it saps its own foundation.

Is there no way to prevent this? Must it continue among Christian people? Allowing that diligence and frugality must produce riches, is there no way to hinder riches from destroying the religion of those who possess them? I can see only one possible way. If you earn all you can and save all you can, you must, in the nature of things, grow rich. Then, if you have any desire to escape the damnation of hell, give all you can, otherwise I can have no more hope of your salvation than that of Judas Iscariot.

I call to God to record upon my soul that I advise no more than I practice. I do, blessed be God, earn and save and give—all I can. This, I trust in God, I shall continue to do while the breath of God is in my nostrils. But what then? I count all things but loss for the excellency of the knowledge of Jesus my Lord! Still, "I give up every plea beside, Lord, I am damn'd! but Thou hast died!"

11

*The Signs of the Times**

*Ye can discern the face of the sky; but can ye not discern
the signs of the times? (Matthew 16:3)*

The entire passage reads, "The Pharisees also with the
Sadducees came, and tempting desired him that he would
show them a sign from heaven. He answered and said unto
them, When it is evening, ye say, It will be fair weather:
for the sky is red. And in the morning, It will be foul
weather today: for the sky is red and lowering. O ye hypocrites, ye can discern the face of the sky; but can ye not
discern the signs of the times?"

"The Pharisees also with the Sadducees came." In general, these two sects were quite opposite, but it is common
for the sinners of the world to stop fighting one another,
at least for a while, to unite in opposing the godly.

"And tempting," testing whether He was, indeed, sent
from God, "desired him that he would show them a sign
from heaven," which they believed no false prophet was
able to do. A sign, they imagined, would convince them

**Op. cit.*, Sermon LXXI, Vol. 2, pp. 93–98.

Jesus was really sent from God.

"He answered and said unto them, When it is evening, ye say, It will be fair weather: for the sky is red. And in the morning, It will be foul weather today: for the sky is red and lowering. Oh ye hypocrites," professing love while you have enmity in your hearts, "ye can discern the face of the sky," and judge by that what the weather will be, "but can ye not discern the signs of the times," when God brings His Son into the world?

Let us think about this. What were the times of which our Lord speaks? What were the signs by which those times were to be distinguished from all others? We may also wonder what are the times which we have reason to believe are now at hand, and how it is that all who are called Christians do not discern the signs of these times.

The time Jesus speaks of is the time of the Messiah, the time ordained before the foundation of the world. It is the time when God gave His only begotten Son to take our nature upon Him and become man. It is the time when He chose to live a life of sorrow and pain, and finally, to be obedient unto death, even the death of the cross, so that whoever believed in Him should not perish but have everlasting life. This was the important time, and the Pharisees and Sadducees could not discern the signs. A thick veil was upon the hearts of these men and they could not discern the tokens of His coming, even though it was foretold long before.

The Signs of Jesus' Coming

What were the signs of the Lord's coming which had been so long and so clearly foretold, giving them insight to discern the times, had not the veil been on their hearts? There were many, but we will mention only a few. One of the first was pointed out in the solemn words of Jacob, shortly before his death, "The scepter shall not depart from Judah, nor a lawgiver from between his feet, until Shiloh come." Both ancient and modern Jews agree that by Shiloh we are to understand the Messiah who was to come, according to the prophecy, before the scepter or the sovereignty departed from Judah. But it did, as everyone agrees, depart from Judah at this very time (the death of Herod the Great), giving them an infallible sign that at this very time Shiloh, or the Messiah, had come.

A second eminent sign of those times, the times of the coming of the Messiah, is given us in the third chapter of the prophecy of Malachi: "Behold, I will send my messenger, and he shall prepare the way before me: and the Lord, whom ye seek, shall suddenly come to his temple." This was fulfilled by the coming of John the Baptist, and then by Jesus himself, coming suddenly to His temple. What sign could be clearer to anyone who impartially considered the words of the prophet Isaiah, "The voice of him that crieth in the wilderness, Prepare ye the way of the Lord, make straight in the desert a highway for our God."

Even clearer signs than these, if any could be clearer, were the mighty works He did. He himself declares, "The works that I do in my Father's name they testify of me." And to these he explicitly refers in His answer to John the Baptist's question, asking if He was the Messiah or if they should look for someone else. No bare verbal answer could have been as convincing as what they saw with their own eyes. Jesus answered, "Go, and show John again those things which ye do hear and see: the blind receive their sight, and the lame walk, the lepers are cleansed, and the deaf hear, the dead are raised up, and the poor have the gospel preached to them."

Then how did it happen that those who were so sharp-sighted in other things and who could read the face of the sky were not able to discern those signs which indicated the coming of the Messiah? They could not discern them, not for lack of evidence, as this was full and clear, but for lack of personal integrity. They were a wicked and adulterous generation, and the perverseness of their hearts spread a cloud over their understanding. Therefore, although the Sun of Righteousness shone bright, they were unaware of this. They were not willing to be convinced, therefore they remained in ignorance. The light was sufficient but they shut their eyes and would not see it. They had no excuse and just retribution fell upon them.

The Signs of Our Times

Our second consideration is, what are the times which we have reason to believe are now at hand, and how is it that all those claiming to be Christians do not discern the signs of these times? The times we believe are at hand, if they have not already begun, are what many pious men have called the time of the latter day glory. This is the time when God will gloriously display His power and love in the fulfillment of His gracious promise that the knowledge of the Lord shall cover the earth as the waters cover the sea. Are there, in any part of the world, any signs of such a time approaching?

Not many years ago an English bishop wrote in a pastoral letter, "I cannot imagine what persons mean, by talking of a great work of God at this time. I do not see any work of God now, more than He has done at any other time."

I believe that he did not see any extraordinary work of God. Neither he nor Christians in general saw any signs of the glorious day that is approaching. How is it that those who can now "discern the face of the sky," who are not only great philosophers but great theologians, as eminent as the Sadducees or the Pharisees ever were, do not discern the signs of those glorious times which, if not begun, are knocking at the door?

We admit, indeed, that in every age of the church, the kingdom of God did not come with observation, with splendor and pomp, or with any of the outward circumstances which usually attend the kingdoms of the world. We know this kingdom of God is within us and that when it begins, either in an individual or in a nation, it is like a grain of mustard seed which at first is the smallest of all seeds. Nevertheless, it gradually increases until it becomes a great tree. To use the comparison of our Lord, it is like a little leaven which a woman took and hid in three measures of meal until the whole was leavened.

We may well ask if there are now any signs that the day of God's power is approaching. I appeal to every candid, unprejudiced person to observe all those same spiritual signs which our Lord mentioned to John's disciples.

"The blind receive their sight." Those who were blinded by sin from birth, unable to see their own deplorable state much less the glory of God and the remedy He has prepared for them in the Son of His love, now see. They see themselves and the light of the glory of God in the face of Jesus Christ. The eyes of their understanding are now opened and they can see all things clearly.

"The deaf hear." Those who were utterly deaf to all the outward and inward calls from God, now hear not only His providential calls but also the whispers of His grace.

"The lame walk." Those who never before arose from the earth or moved one step toward heaven, are now walking in all the ways of God and running the race that is set before them.

"The lepers are cleansed." The deadly leprosy of sin which no work of man could ever cure is now gone from them. Surely, never in any age or nation since the apostles have those words been so completely fulfilled.

"The poor have the gospel preached to them," as it is at this day. The gospel leaven—faith working by love, inward and outward holiness, righteousness, peace and joy in the Holy Spirit—has spread throughout various parts of the world. Sinners have been truly converted to God, thoroughly changed both in heart and in life, by the thousands. This fact cannot be denied. We can show the persons and give their names and addresses. Yet the so-called wise men of the world, men of distinction, learning and renown, cannot imagine what we mean by talking of any extraordinary work of God.

Sin Prevents Seeing the Signs

They cannot discern the signs of these times. They can see no sign at all of God's arising to maintain His own cause and set up His kingdom over the earth. How is it that they cannot discern the signs of these times? We may account for their lack of discernment on the same principle we accounted for that of the Pharisees and Sadducees. They, also, are what those were, an adulterous and sinful generation. If their eye was single, their whole body would be full of light; but if evil, their whole body must be full of darkness. Every evil thought darkens the soul, every evil passion clouds the understanding. It follows we cannot expect them to be able to discern the signs of the times if they are full of all disorderly passions and slaves to every evil temper.

They are full of pride, thinking of themselves far more highly than they ought. They are vain, seeking honor from one another. This is not the honor that comes from God alone. They cherish hatred and malice in their hearts. They give in to anger, envy, and revenge. They return evil for evil, insults for insults, and accusations for accusations. Instead of overcoming evil with good, they do not hesitate to demand an eye for an eye and a tooth for a tooth. They do not savor the things of God but the things of men. They set their affections not on things above but on the things of earth. They love the creature more than the Creator. They are lovers of pleasure more than lovers of God. How, then, can they discern the signs of the times? Satan, the god of this world, has blinded their hearts and covered their minds with a veil of thick darkness. What have these souls of flesh and blood to do with God or the things of God?

John gives this very reason for the Jews not understanding the things of God. Because of their preceding sins and willful rejection of the light, God delivered them to Satan, who blinded them beyond recovery. Over and over, when they might have seen, they would not. They shut their eyes against the light and now they cannot see. God gave them up to an undiscerning mind, so they do not believe. John quoted from Isaiah: "He hath blinded their eyes, and hardened their hearts; that they should not see with their eyes, nor understand with their heart, and be converted, and I should heal them." The plain meaning is not that God did this by His own immediate power. It would be blasphemy to say that God, in this sense, hardens any man, but His Spirit strives with them no longer and Satan hardens them effectively.

As it was with them in ancient times, so it is with the present generation. Thousands of those who claim the name "Christian" are now given up to an undiscerning mind. Satan has so blinded their eyes that light cannot shine upon them, so they can no more discern the signs of the times than the Pharisees and Sadducees could of old.

An instance of this spiritual blindness, this total inability to discern the signs of the times mentioned in Scripture, is in the work of an eminent writer who thought the New Jerusalem came down from heaven when Constantine the Great called himself a Christian and legalized Christianity.

By the same rule, what signs would this writer have expected of the approaching conversion of the pagans? He would undoubtedly have expected a hero, like Charles of Sweden or Frederick of Prussia, to carry fire and sword and Christianity through whole nations at once. It is true, since the time of Constantine, that many nations have been converted in this way. But it cannot be said about conversions like these, "The kingdom of heaven cometh not with observation," because everyone would see a warrior rushing through the land with fifty or sixty thousand men behind.

However, this is not the way the Author of Christianity, the Prince of Peace, has chosen to spread His gospel. This is not the manner in which a grain of mustard seed grows up into a great tree. It is not the way a little leaven leavens the whole loaf. We may form a judgment of what will be hereafter by what we have already seen. This is the way true Christianity, the faith that works by love, has been spreading.

It continues to spread in the same manner now. This may easily be seen by all whose eyes are not blind. All those who experience in their own hearts God's power of salvation will readily see how the same religion which they enjoy is still spreading from heart to heart. They know of the same grace of God working strongly and sweetly everywhere. They rejoice in finding another sinner asking, "What must I do to be saved?" Their answer is, "My soul doth magnify the Lord, and my spirit hath rejoiced in God my Savior." Upon fair and candid inquiry, they find not only those who had some form of religion, but those who had none at all and were lost, abandoned sinners, all now entirely changed, truly fearing God and working in righteousness. They observe more and more of these former outcasts who are inwardly and outwardly changed, loving God and their neighbor, living in the practice of justice, mercy, and truth, doing good to all men, easy and happy in their lives, and triumphant in their death.

There is no excuse, then, for any of us who believe Scripture to be the Word of God, not to discern the signs of these times as preparatory to the general call of the irreligious. What more could God have done to convince us that the day is coming and the time at hand when He will fulfill His glorious promises and arise to maintain His own cause and set up His kingdom over all the earth? What, indeed, unless He had forced us to believe? This He could not do without destroying the nature which He had given us. He made us free beings with the inward power of self-determination. He deals with us as free beings, from first to last.

As a free being, you may open or shut your eyes as you please. You have sufficient light shining all around you, yet you need not see it unless you will. Be assured God is not well pleased with your shutting your eyes and then saying, "I cannot see." I advise you to make a careful and honest examination of all this.

After a candid, personal inquiry into the matter, consider carefully what God has wrought. Who has seen or heard such a thing? Has a nation been "born in a day"? Consider how swift, as well as how deep, and how extensive a work has been done in the present age, not by secular might or power, but by the Spirit of the Lord. How utterly inadequate were the means and how insufficient the instruments to work such an effect as it has pleased God to allow in Great Britain and America. God has always worked with unlikely instruments from the very beginning. "A few young raw heads," said the Bishop of London, "what can they pretend to do?" They "pretended," or claimed, only to be instuments in the hand of God. They "pretended" only to do the work God had given them to do, to do just what the Lord pleased. If it is His pleasure to throw down the walls of Jericho, the strongholds of Satan, not by the effects of war but by the blasts of rams' horns, who shall ask Him, "What doest Thou?"

Meantime, your eyes are blessed for they see. Many prophets and righteous men have desired to see the things you see and have not seen them, and to hear the things you hear and have not heard them. You see and acknowledge the day of your visitation, such a visitation as neither you nor your forefathers had known. You may well say, "This is the day which the Lord hath made; we will rejoice and be glad in it." This is the dawn of that glorious day of which all the prophets have spoken. How will you utilize this opportunity you have?

See that you do not receive the blessing of God in vain. Begin at the root, if you have not already. Now repent and believe the gospel. If you have believed, look to yourselves that you do not lose what you have wrought, but that you receive a full reward. Stir up the gift of God that is within you. Walk in the light as He is in the light. While you hold fast to what you have attained, go on to perfection. When you are made perfect in love, forget the things that are behind and press on to the mark, for the prize of the high calling of God in Christ Jesus.

Help your neighbors. "Let your light so shine before men, that they may see your good works, and glorify your Father which is in heaven." Do good to all men, but especially to those who are of the household of faith. Proclaim the glad tidings of salvation, not only to those of your household, not only to your relations, friends, and acquaintances, but to all whom God providentially delivers into your hands. You, who already know in whom you believe, are the salt of the earth. Work to season everyone you meet with the knowledge and love of God. You are as a city set upon a hill and you must not be hidden. You are the light of the world. Men do not light a candle and put it under a bushel, so our all wise God surely will not. Let your light shine to all who are in the house, to all who witness your life and conversation. Above all, continue earnestly in prayer, both for yourselves, for all the church of God and for all the children of men. Pray that they may remember themselves and be turned to our God, and that they may also enjoy the gospel blessing on earth and the glory of God in heaven.

12

*The Great Judgment**

*We shall all stand before the judgment seat of Christ.
(Romans 14:10)*

· How many circumstances concur to raise before us the
awfulness of this solemn scripture, for we shall all stand
before the judgment seat of Christ. "For as I live," Jesus
said, "every knee shall bow to me, and every tongue shall
confess to God." In that day, every one of us shall give
account of himself to God. Little else could strengthen our
hands to do good and deter us from all evil than a strong
conviction that the Judge is standing at the door and we
are shortly to stand before Him.

If all men had a deep understanding of this, it would
very effectively protect the interests of society. No better
motive can be found to guarantee a steady pursuit of solid
virtue and a uniform walk in justice, mercy, and truth.

It is, therefore, proper and suitable to consider three
important factors. These are the chief circumstances
which will precede our standing before the judgment seat

Op. cit., Sermon XV, Vol.1, pp. 126–134.

of Christ, the judgment itself, and a few of the circumstances which will follow it.

Before the Judgment

Let us first consider the chief circumstances which will precede our standing before the judgment seat of Christ. God will show signs in the earth. He will arise to "shake terribly the earth." "The earth shall reel to and fro like a drunkard, and shall be removed like a cottage." There will be earthquakes, not only in a few different places but in all places, in every part of the habitable world. Revelation tells us, "Such as was not since men were upon the earth, so mighty an earthquake and so great." In one of these, every island will disappear and the mountains will crumble.

Meantime, all the waters of the surface of the earth will feel the violence of those concussions. The sea and waves will roar with an agitation as has never been known since the fountains of the great deep were broken up to flood and destroy the earth. The air will be all storm and tempest, full of dark vapors and pillars of smoke. Thunder will resound from pole to pole, flashing with ten thousand lightning bolts.

The commotion will not stop in the region of the air. The powers of heaven also will be shaken. There will be signs in the sun and in the moon and in the stars. The sun will be turned to darkness and the moon into blood before the great and terrible day of the Lord comes. The stars will stop shining and fall from heaven. Then the universal shout from all the companies of heaven will be heard, followed by the voice of the archangel proclaiming the approach of the Son of God. The trumpet of God will sound an alarm to all the dead. All the graves will open and the bodies of men will arise. The sea will also give up its dead and everyone will rise with a body changed beyond our imagination.

"For this corruptible must put on incorruption, and this mortal must put on immortality." Yes, death and hell, the invisible world, will deliver up the dead that are in them, so that everyone who has ever lived and died since God created man will be raised, incorruptible and immortal.

At the same time, Jesus will send forth His angels over all the earth and they will gather His elect from the four winds, from one end of heaven to the other. Then He will come with clouds, in His own glory and the glory of His Father, with ten thousand of His saints and myriads of angels, and will sit on the throne of His glory. All the nations will sit before Him and He will separate them one from another, with the good sheep on His right hand and the wicked goats on His left.

. John wrote about this general assembly, saying he saw all who had been dead, standing before God, and all the books were open. The dead were being judged from the things written in the books about what each had done or left undone. These are the chief circumstances recorded in God's prophecies which will precede the general judgment.

The Judgment

Now let us consider the judgment itself, as God has revealed it. The person by whom God will judge the world is His only begotten Son, whose goings forth are from everlasting and who is God over all, blessed forever. To Him who is the radiance of His Father's glory, the express image of His person, the Father has given all judgment, because He is the Son of Man. Although He was in the form of God and equal with God, He emptied himself and took on the form of a servant, the likeness of men. As a man, He humbled himself even more, becoming obedient unto death, even the death of the cross. Because of this, God has highly exalted Him, even in His human nature, and ordained Him, as a man, to be the judge of the quick and the dead, those who are still alive when He comes and those who are dead.

The time known as the great and terrible day is usually called in Scripture, "the day of the Lord." The time from the creation of man upon the earth to the end of all things is the day of the sons of men. The time that is now passing over us is known as our day. When this is ended, the day of the Lord will begin. Who can say how long it will continue? With the Lord one day is as a thousand years and a thousand years as one day. From this expression, some of the early Christians drew the inference that what is commonly called the day of judgment would be, indeed, a thousand years. It seems they did not go beyond the truth or examine that expression. If we consider the number of persons who are to be judged and the actions to be inquired into, it does not appear that a thousand years will suffice for the transactions of that day. It may comprise several thousand years, but God will reveal this, also, in its season.

We have no explicit account in Scripture regarding the place where mankind will be judged. Many think it will be on the earth, where the works to be judged were done, and that God will employ His angels, "To smooth and lengthen out the boundless space, and spread an area for all human race."

Perhaps it agrees more with Jesus' own account of His coming in the clouds, to think it will be above the earth. This supposition is favored by what Paul wrote to the Thessalonians, "The dead in Christ shall rise first. Then we which are alive and remain shall be caught up together with them in the clouds, to meet the Lord in the air." So it seems to me most probable Jesus' great white throne will be high exalted above the earth.

No one can count the persons to be judged, any more than the drops of rain or the sands of the sea. John said he beheld a great multitude which no man can number, clothed in white robes with palms in their hands. How immense the total multitude must be—with all nations, and kindreds, and people, and tongues, all who have sprung from the loins of Adam, from the beginning of the world to the end of time. What a congregation all those thousands of years of generations must make when we realize that the earth is populated at any one time by millions of living souls.

Every man, woman, and child who ever breathed will then hear the voice of the Son of God and appear before Him. This seems to be the meaning of the expression, "the dead, small and great" includes all universally; all without exception; all of every age, sex, or degree; all who ever lived and died. For long before that day the phantom of human greatness disappears and sinks into nothing. Even in the moment of death, all that vanishes away. Who is rich in the grave?

There, every man shall give an account of his own works, a full and true account of all that he ever did while alive, whether it was good or evil. What a scene will then be disclosed in the sight of angels and men as ordained by the Lord God Almighty, who knows all things in heaven and in earth.

Not only will all the *actions* of every person be then brought to open view, but all their *words*. Every idle word which has been spoken shall be called into account in the day of judgment. So, by words as well as works, each man will be justified or condemned.

God will then bring to light every circumstance that

accompanied each word and action. He will judge whether they lessened or increased the goodness or badness of them. How easy this is for Him who is about our home and about our path and who sees all our ways. We know the darkness is not darkness to Him, but the night shines as bright as day. He will bring to light not only the hidden works of darkness but the very thoughts and intents of the heart, for He "searcheth the reins and hearts." All things are naked and open to the eyes of God to whom we have to answer. Hell and destruction are before Him without a covering. How much more open are the hearts of men?

In that day, every inward working of the human soul will be discovered—every appetite, passion, inclination, and affection, with all the various combinations of them, and every temper and disposition that constitute the whole complex character of each individual. Who was righteous, who was unrighteous, and in what degree every action, or person, or character was either good or evil will be seen clearly and infallibly.

Then Jesus will say to those on His right hand, "Come, ye blessed of my Father. . . . For I was an hungered, and ye gave me meat: I was thirsty, and ye gave me drink: I was a stranger, and ye took me in; naked, and ye clothed me." In the same way, all the good they did on earth will be recited before men and angels, whatever they had done either in word or deed, in the name or for the sake of the Lord Jesus. All their good desires, intentions, thoughts, and all their holy dispositions will also be remembered, and it will appear that though they were unknown or forgotten among men, yet God noted them in His book. All their sufferings for the name of Christ and for the testimony of a good conscience will be displayed to their praise from the righteous Judge, their honor before saints and angels, and the increase of that far more exceeding and eternal weight of glory.

Their evil deeds, too, will be remembered on that day and mentioned in the great congregation, as there is not a person alive who has not sinned once in his entire life.

Many do not believe this and ask, "Would not this imply that their sufferings were not at an end, even when life ended, as they would still have sorrow and shame and confusion of face to endure? How can this be reconciled with God's declaration through Ezekiel, 'If the wicked will turn from all his sins that he hath committed, and keep all my statutes, and do that which is lawful and right. . . all his transgressions that he hath committed, they shall not be mentioned unto him.' How is it consistent with the promise which God made to all who accept the gospel covenant, 'I will forgive their iniquity, and I will remember their sin no more,' or, as the letter to the Hebrews says, 'I will be merciful to their unrighteousness, and their sins and iniquities will I remember no more'?"

. This is the answer to their questions. It is apparently and absolutely necessary for the full display of the glory of God, and the clear and perfect manifestation of His wisdom, justice, power, and mercy toward the heirs of salvation. All the circumstances of their lives must be placed in full view, together with all their tempers and all the desires, thoughts and intents of their hearts. Otherwise, it would not appear that the grace of God has delivered them out of a depth of sin and misery. Indeed, if the whole lives of all the children of men were not manifestly discovered, the whole amazing fabric of divine providence could not be manifested nor would we be able in a thousand instances to justify the ways of God to man. Unless our Lord's words were fulfilled in their fullest sense, without any restriction or limitation, "There is nothing covered that shall not be revealed; and hid, that shall not be known," the abundance of God's dispensations would still appear without their reasons. Then, only when God has brought to light all the hidden things of darkness, it will be seen that all His ways were wise and good, that He saw through the thick cloud and governed all things by the wise counsel of His own will, and that nothing was left to chance or the whims of man. Then it will be seen that God disposed all strongly and sweetly and wrought everything into one connected chain of justice, mercy, and truth.

In the discovery of the divine perfections, the righteous will rejoice with unspeakable joy. They will not feel any painful sorrow or shame for any of those past transgressions which were long since blotted out and washed away by the blood of the Lamb. It will be enough for them that none of the transgressions which they had committed will ever be mentioned to them for any disadvantage. Their sins and iniquities will not be remembered to condemn them. This is the plain meaning of the promise, and all the children of God will find it true to their everlasting comfort.

After the righteous are judged, Jesus will turn to those on His left hand and they will be judged, also, every man according to his works. Not only their outward works will be brought into account, but all the evil words which they had ever spoken, all the evil desires, affections, and tempers which had a place in their souls, and all the evil thoughts or designs which were ever cherished in their hearts. The joyful sentence of acquittal will then be pronounced upon those on the right hand, and the dreadful sentence of condemnation upon those on the left hand. Both of these sentences must remain as fixed and unmovable as the throne of God.

After the Judgment

We should now consider a few of the circumstances which will follow the general judgment. The first is the execution of the sentences pronounced on the evil and on the good. The evil will go away into eternal punishment, and the righteous into life eternal. It should be observed the very same word is used in both sentences. It follows that either the punishment will last forever or the reward, too, will come to an end. This could never be, unless God could come to an end or His mercy and truth could fail. Scripture tells us the righteous will shine forth as the sun in the kingdom of the Father and will drink of the rivers of pleasure which are at God's right hand forever. Here all description falls short and all human language fails. Only one who is caught up into the third heaven can have any conception of it, but even such a one cannot express what he has seen. It is impossible for man to utter words about these things.

The wicked, meantime, including all those who forgot God, will be sent to hell. They will be punished with everlasting destruction from the presence of the Lord and from the glory of His power. They will be cast into the lake of fire burning with brimstone, originally prepared for the devil and his angels, where they will anguish in pain. They will curse God and look upward. There the dogs of hell—pride, malice, revenge, rage, horror, and despair will continually devour them. They will have no rest, day or night, but the smoke of their torment will ascend for ever and ever. "Their worm dieth not, and the fire is not quenched."

Then the heavens will be shriveled up as a parchment scroll and pass away with a great noise. They will flee from the face of Him who sits on the throne and no place will be found for them. The very manner of their passing away is disclosed to us by Peter, "The heavens being on fire shall be dissolved." The whole beautiful fabric will be overthrown by that raging element and the connection of all its parts destroyed. Every atom will be torn away from every other atom. The earth, also, and all the works in it will be burned up.

The enormous works of nature, the everlasting hills and mountains that have defied the erosion of time and stood unmoved so many thousand years, will sink down in fiery ruin. How much less will man's sturdiest works of art, such as tombs, pillars, arches, castles, and pyramids, the utmost effort of human industry, be able to withstand the flaming conqueror. All will die, perish, vanish away like a dream.

Some think it requires the same Almighty Power to annihilate things as it required to create them, and that no atom in the universe will be totally or finally destroyed. Since glass is produced from intense heat, the whole earth, if not the heavens also, will undergo this change, after which the fire will have no further power. Those believe this is intimated in the revelation made to John, "Before the throne there was a sea of glass like unto crystal."

There is one more circumstance which will follow the judgment that deserves our serious consideration. Peter says, "We, according to His promise, look for new heavens and a new earth, wherein dwelleth righteousness." The promise stands in the prophecy of Isaiah, "Behold, I create new heavens and a new earth: and the former shall not be remembered." John saw them in the visions of God. "I saw," he said, "a new heaven and a new earth, for the first heaven and the first earth were passed away." And only righteousness dwelt therein. He added that he heard a great voice from the third heaven, saying, "Behold the tabernacle of God is with men, and he will dwell with them, and they shall be his people, and God himself shall be with them, and be their God!" Of necessity, therefore, they will all be happy. God will wipe away all the tears from their eyes and there will be no more death or sorrow or crying or pain or curse. They will see His face and have the nearest access to Him and the highest resemblance of Him.

Lessons For Life

It remains only to apply the preceding considerations to all who are here before God. We are directly led to do so by these events which so naturally point us to that day when the Lord will judge the world in righteousness. This, by reminding us of that more awful time, may furnish many lessons of instruction. May God write them on all our hearts.

First, how beautiful are the feet of those who are sent by the wise and gracious providence of God to execute justice on earth, to defend the injured, and punish the wrongdoer. They are the ministers of God to us for good, the grand supporters of the public tranquility, the patrons of innocence and virtue, the great security of all our worldly blessings. Every one of these represents not only an earthly prince but the Judge of the earth, Him whose name is written on His thigh, King of Kings and Lord of Lords. Oh that all the sons of the right hand of the Most High may be holy as He is holy, wise with the wisdom that sits by His throne, like Him who is the eternal wisdom of the Father. May they not be respecters of persons as He is not, but rendering to every man according to his works, inflexibly, inexorably just, though full of pity and of tender mercy like Him. Then they will be terrible, indeed, to those who do evil. So shall the laws of our land have their full use and due honor, and the throne of our King will be established in righteousness.

You truly honorable men, whom God and the king have commissioned in a lower degree to administer justice, may be compared to those ministering spirits who will attend the Judge coming in the clouds. Like them, be filled with love for God and man. Love righteousness and hate iniquity. Minister in your several spheres to those who will be heirs of salvation and to the glory of God. Remain the establishers of peace, the blessing and ornaments of your country, the protectors of a guilty world, and the guardian angels of all who are around you.

You, whose duty it is to execute what is given you by the Judge before whom you stand, how nearly you are concerned to resemble those who stand before the face of the Son of man, those servants of His who do His pleasure and hearken to the voice of His words. You must be incorrupt, just, and love mercy, and do to others as you would have others do to you; so your great Judge, under whose eye you continually stand, will say to you, "Well done, thou good and faithful servant, enter thou into the joy of thy Lord!"

Allow me to add a few words to all of you who are at this day present before the Lord. You should bear in mind that a more awful day is coming. This is a large assembly, but it is nothing to the general assembly of all the children of men who ever lived on earth. A few will stand at the judgment seat today, to be judged on the charges laid against them. They are now in prison, perhaps in chains, until they are brought forth to be tried and sentenced. But we shall all, I who speak and you who hear, stand at the judgment seat of Christ. We are now on this earth, which is not our home, in this prison of flesh and blood, and perhaps many of us are in chains of darkness, waiting to be brought forth. Here, a man is questioned about one or two deeds he is alleged to have committed. There, we are to give a full account of all our works from the cradle to the grave, all words, desires and tempers, all thoughts and intents of our hearts. God said, "Give an account of thy stewardship, for thou mayest be no longer steward," and we must account for all the use we have made of our various talents—whether of mind, body, or fortune.

In worldly courts it is possible some who are guilty may be freed for lack of evidence, but there is no lack of evidence in God's court. All those you have had dealings with, secret or otherwise, all those who know your schemes, plans, and actions, are ready to face you. So are all the spirits of darkness, who inspired evil designs and assisted in the execution of them. So are all the angels of God, those eyes of the Lord who run over all the earth, who watched over your soul and labored for your good, as much as you would permit. So is your own conscience, a thousand witnesses in one, no more capable of being either blinded or silenced, but constrained to know and to speak the naked truth about all your thoughts and words and actions. If conscience is a thousand witnesses, God is a thousand consciences. Oh, who can stand before the face of our great God, even our Savior, Jesus Christ.

You cannot escape the final judgment. You will beg the mountains to fall on you and the rocks to cover you, but the mountains, the rocks, the earth and the heavens are ready to flee away. You cannot prevent the sentence, not with all the substance of your house, with thousands in gold and silver.

You came naked from your mother's womb and you will go more naked into eternity. Hear the Lord, the Judge, "Come ye blessed of My Father, inherit the kingdom prepared for you from the foundation of the world." What a joyful sound. How very different from that voice which echoes throughout heaven, "Depart from me, ye cursed, into everlasting fire, prepared for the devil and his angels!" There is no one who can prevent or retard the full execution of either sentence. Hell is moved from beneath to receive those who are ripe for destruction, while the everlasting doors lift up their heads that the heirs of glory may come in.

Knowing this day will come, we should be holy in word and deed. Be diligent that you may be found blameless and without spot. We know it cannot be long before the Lord will descend with the voice of the archangel and the trumpet of God. He will come and will not tarry. Then, every one of us will appear before Him and give account of our own works. He wants all of us to come to repentance, to faith in a bleeding Lord, to spotless love, to the full image of God, renewed in the heart and producing all holiness of conversation. He does not want any of us to be found on His left hand—to perish. Remember, the Judge of all is also the Savior of all. He has bought us with His own blood that we might not perish but have everlasting life. Prove His mercy rather than His justice. Claim His love rather than the thunder of His power. He is not far from every one of us. He is coming, not to condemn, but to save the world. He stands in our midst. Sinners, even now He knocks at the doors of your hearts. Give yourselves to Him who gave himself for you in humble faith, in holy, active, patient love. Rejoice with exceeding joy in His day, when He comes in the clouds of heaven.

13

*The General Salvation**

The earnest expectation of the creature waiteth for the manifestation of the sons of God. For the creature was made subject to vanity, not willingly, but by reason of him who hath subjected the same in hope, because the creature itself also shall be delivered from the bondage of corruption into the glorious liberty of the children of God. For we know that the whole creation groaneth and travaileth in pain together until now. (Romans 8:19–22)

Nothing is more sure than the Lord's love to every man. His mercy is over all His works, especially all that have sense and are capable of pleasure, pain, happiness or misery. Because of this, He opens His hand and abundantly fills all living things. He prepares food for animals and for men. He provides for the birds of the air, feeding them when they cry to Him. He sends springs into the rivers so every creature may drink. He directs us to be tender and to show mercy to every creature, saying, "Thou shalt not muzzle the ox that treadeth out the corn." Paul asks if God

Op. cit., Sermon LXV, Vol.2, pp. 49–56.

cares for oxen. He undoubtedly does, and we cannot deny it without flatly contradicting His Word. There is more implied in the text. We are to feed the bodies of those whom we desire to feed our souls.

Are these scriptures confirmed by the present state of things? Are they consistent with what we daily see around us in every part of creation? If the Creator and Father of every living thing is rich in mercy toward all, if He does not overlook or disdain any of the works of His own hands, if He wills even the lowest of them to be happy according to their ability, why is everything subject to the complications of evil, even to the point of being overwhelmed by it? How is it that all kinds of misery are widespread over the face of the earth? This is a question which has puzzled the wisest philosophers in all ages and it cannot be answered without studying the prophecies of God.

Using His prophecies as our guide, we may study the original, the present, and the future state of creation at the manifestation of God's children.

Paradise Revisited

In the first place, we learn of the original state from the place assigned to them, God's garden. All the beasts and all the birds were with Adam in paradise. There is no question that their state was suited to their place. They were perfectly happy. Taking a short view of one shows us the other. Man was made in the image of God. God is a Spirit, and so was man, except that man's spirit was designed to dwell on earth, lodged in an earthly body. As such, he had the ability to move on his own, as has every spirit in the universe. This is the distinction between spirit and passive matter.

In the likeness of his Creator, man was endued with understanding, able to understand and judge whatever objects were brought before him. Man was given a will, exerting itself in various affections and passions. He was endued with freedom of choice. Without that free will, all the rest would have been in vain and he would have been as incapable of serving his Creator as a slab of marble. He would have been as incapable of vice or virtue as any part of the inanimate creation. The image of God in man consisted of the power of spontaneous motion, understanding, will, and freedom of choice.

We cannot determine how far man's power of self-motion extended at that time. It is probable he had far more swiftness and strength than any of his descendants or any of the lower creatures ever had. It is certain he had more strength of understanding than any man following. His understanding was perfect for him. He was capable of seeing all things clearly and judging them according to truth, without any mixture of error. His will had no wrong bias of any sort and all his thoughts and feelings were right, being guided by the dictates of perfect understanding. He embraced nothing but good, and every good in proportion to its degree of intrinsic goodness. His freedom of choice was also wholly guided by his understanding, and he chose or rejected according to its direction. Above all, he was a creature of God. He was capable of knowing, loving, and obeying his Creator. In fact, he did know God and sincerely loved and invariably obeyed Him. This was the supreme perfection of man, as it is of all intelligent beings, to continually see, love, and obey God our Father. From the right state and right use of all his faculties, his happiness naturally flowed. This was the essence of his happiness, but it was increased by all the things that were around him. He saw, with unspeakable pleasure, the order, beauty, and harmony of all creatures. He enjoyed the serenity of the skies, the brightness of the sun, the sweetly variegated colors of the earth, the trees, the fruits, the flowers, and the sights and sounds of all the waters.

This pleasure was not marred by evil of any kind. There was no dilution by any sorrow or pain of either mind or body. While man was innocent, he was impassive, incapable of suffering, and nothing could stain his pure joy. The crowning touch: he was immortal.

To this creature, endowed with all these excellent faculties, thus qualifying him for his high calling, God gave "dominion over the fish of the sea, and over the fowl of the air . . . and over every creeping thing that creepeth upon the earth." The Psalmist also said, "Thou madest him to have dominion over the works of thy hands; thou hast put all things under his feet: all sheep and oxen, yea, and the beasts of the field; the fowl of the air, and the fish of the sea, and whatsoever passeth through the paths of the seas."

So man was God's vice-regent on earth, the prince and governor of this lower world—all His blessings flowing through man to the lesser creatures. Man was the channel of conveyance between his Creator and the whole creation.

We must look to see what blessings were conveyed through man to the lower creatures and what was the original state of these brute creatures when they were first created. This deserves more careful consideration than is usually given it. It is certain these creatures, as well as man, had the ability to move on their own, at least as much as they have today. They were given a degree of understanding, no less than they have now. They also had a will, including various passions which they still have. They had power of choice, a degree of which is still found in every living creature. We cannot doubt that their understanding, too, in the beginning, was perfect in its kind. Their passions and affections were regulated by God's natural laws and their choice was always guided by their understanding.

The barrier between men and beasts, the line which they cannot cross, is not reason or understanding. We cannot deny they have this. But man has capabilities that the lower creatures do not have. We have no reason to believe they are, in any degree, capable of knowing, loving, or obeying God. This is the specific difference between man and animal, the great gulf they cannot pass over.

As a loving obedience to God was the perfection of man, so a loving obedience to man was the perfection of animals. As long as they continued in this, they were as happy as their nature allowed, happy in the right state and the right use of their respective faculties. They even had some shadowy resemblance of moral goodness, as they had gratitude to man for benefits received and a reverence for him. They also had a kind of good will toward each other, unmixed with anything contrary.

How beautiful many of them were, we may deduce from those still remaining—both the noblest creatures as well as those of the lowest order. They were surrounded with abundant food and with everything that could give them pleasure. This pleasure was unmixed with pain, as pain had not yet entered paradise. Like man, they, too, were immortal, for God had not made death and He had no pleasure in the death of any living thing. At that time, God saw everything that He had made and it was all very good.

The Effects of the Fall

This is far from being true today. The whole lower world, to say nothing of inanimate nature, seems to be off course and fighting against man. Since man rebelled against God, "The whole creation groaneth and travaileth in pain together until now," as Paul said.

Since all the blessings of God in paradise flowed

through man to the inferior creatures, man was the great channel of communication between the Creator and the whole world. When man made himself incapable of transmitting those blessings, that communication was cut off. Thus, exchange between God and the inferior creatures stopped and His blessings could no longer flow in on them. It was then that every creature was subjected to vanity, sorrow, and pain of every kind, and to all manner of evil. This came not by God's own choice, act or deed, but through man's transgression.

When man rebelled against God, the lower creatures probably sustained great loss in their vigor, strength and swiftness. Undoubtedly they suffered far more in their understanding, much more than we can imagine. Perhaps insects and worms had as much understanding then as the most intelligent of the brutes now have. But now millions of creatures understand little more than the earth on which they crawl or the rock to which they cling.

They suffered still more in their will and their passions, which were then variously distorted and frequently set in flat opposition to the little understanding that was left them. Their liberty was greatly impaired, or in many cases totally destroyed. They are still utterly enslaved to irrational appetites which have full power over them. The very foundations of their nature are turned upside down. As man is deprived of his perfection, his loving obedience to God, so the beasts are deprived of their perfection, their loving obedience to man. Most of them flee from him and studiously avoid his hated presence. Most of the rest of them defy man and some even destroy him if they can. Only the few which we call domestic animals retain more or less of their original disposition, through the mercy of God, and continue to love and obey man. In all others, savage fierceness and unrelenting cruelty became part of their nature.

This, then, is the miserable condition of the world at the present time, that such an immense number of creatures can only preserve their own lives by destroying their fellow creatures.

The outward appearance of many of the creatures of the animal world is as ugly as their dispositions. They have lost the beauty which was stamped on them when they first came out of the hands of their Creator. In many there is not the least trace of beauty left. Some are shocking to behold, all terrible and grisly and quite deformed. Their features, ugly at best, are frequently made more deformed than usual when they are distorted by pains which they cannot avoid. Pains of various kinds, weakness, sickness, disease, come on them, perhaps from within, perhaps from one another, perhaps from the change of the seasons, from fire, hail, snow, storm, or from a thousand causes which they can neither foresee nor prevent.

As by one man sin entered into the world, and death by sin, death was passed upon all. Man was not alone in this, but death was also passed on to all the creatures who did not sin as Adam sinned. With death came all the train of preparatory evils, pain and much suffering. All the deviant passions and disagreeable tempers, which in men are sins and in brutes are sources of misery, were passed on to all the inhabitants of the earth and they remain in all except the children of God.

During this present time of vain pursuit on earth, not only are the feebler creatures continually destroyed by the stronger and the strong destroyed by those of equal strength, but both are exposed to the violence and cruelty of their common enemy, man. If man's swiftness and strength is not equal to theirs, his skill is greater. By this he eludes all their force, however great it is. By this he defeats all their swiftness and discovers all their hiding places. He pursues them over the widest plains and through the thickest forests. He overtakes them in the fields, in the air, and finds them in the depth of the sea. Not even the mild and friendly creatures which are under man's influence and obey his commands are safe from his brutal violence. The generous horse that serves its master's necessity or pleasure with unwearied diligence is whipped. The faithful dog that waits for the motion of his hand or his eye is often kicked. Many of these poor creatures find poor return for their long and faithful service. What a dreadful difference there is between what they suffer from their fellow brutes and from the tyrant man. The lion, tiger, or shark give pain from necessity to prolong their own lives, but the human being, without any necessity, torments them of his own free choice. Where their fellow animals put them out of their pain at once, man may continue their lingering pain for months or years, until death releases them.

Paradise Regained

Will the creature, even the brute creation, always remain in this deplorable condition? God forbid that we should even entertain such a thought. While the whole creation groans together, whether or not men listen, their groans are not lost in the air, but enter the ears of Him who made them. While His creatures labor together in pain, God knows all their pain and is bringing them nearer and nearer to the release which will be accomplished in its season. He sees the earnest expectation of all creation, waiting for that final manifestation of the sons of God when they themselves will be delivered from bondage into a measure of the freedom of the children of God. Nothing can be more certain. God said they will be delivered from the bondage of corruption into a measure of the glorious liberty of the children of God, insofar as they are capable.

A general view of this is given us in the twenty-first chapter of Revelation. When He who sits on the great white throne has pronounced, "Behold, I make all things new," and when "the tabernacle of God is with men . . . and they shall be his people, and God himself shall be with them and be their God," then the great blessing will take place. This blessing will be not only on the children of men but on every creature according to its capacity, for there is no restriction in the text. "God shall wipe away all tears from their eyes; and there shall be no more death, neither sorrow, nor crying, neither shall there be any more pain: for the former things are passed away."

The whole brute creation will then be restored, not only to the vigor, strength and swiftness which they had at their creation, but to a far higher degree of each than they ever enjoyed. They will be restored, not only to the measure of understanding they had in paradise but to a much higher degree. Whatever affections they had in the garden of God will be restored with vast increase, being exalted and refined in a manner which we ourselves are not now able to comprehend. The liberty they once had will be completely restored, so they will be free in all their motions. They will be delivered from all irregular appetites, from all unruly passions, from every disposition that is either evil in itself or has a tendency to evil. No rage will be found in any creature, no fierceness, no cruelty or thirst for blood. The wolf will dwell with the lamb, the leopard will lie down with the kid, the calf and the young lion together in peace, and a little child will lead them. The cow and the bear will feed together and the lion will eat straw like the ox. They will not hurt or destroy in all God's holy mountain.

In that day all the emptiness to which they are now

helplessly subject will be abolished. They will suffer no more—either from within or without. The days of their groaning will end. At the same time, there can be no reasonable doubt but all the ugliness of their appearance and all the deformity of their being will vanish and be exchanged for their primeval beauty. With their beauty, their happiness will return. There will be nothing within or without to give them any uneasiness, no heat or cold, no storm or tempest, just a perennial spring.

In the new earth, as well as the new heavens, there will be nothing to give pain, but everything that the wisdom and goodness of God can create to give happiness. As a recompense for what they suffered while under the bondage of corruption, they will enjoy unending happiness suited to their state when God has renewed the face of the earth and their corruptible bodies have become incorruptible.

I have no doubt that the Father of all has a tender regard for even His lowest creatures, so He will make amends for all they suffer while under their present bondage, but I cannot say He has an equal regard for them and the children of men. I do not believe "He sees with equal eyes, as Lord of all, a hero perish, or a sparrow fall." This is very pretty, but absolutely false, for it is also said,

"Mercy, with truth and endless grace,
O'er all His works doth reign,
Yet chiefly He delights to bless His favorite creature,
man."

God has great regard for the least of His creatures, but He regards man much more. He does not equally regard a hero and a sparrow or the best of men and the lowest of beasts. "How much more does your heavenly Father care for you," Jesus said. Those who pushed the point were clearly answered by His question, "Are ye not much better than they?" God regards everything that He has made in its own order and in proportion to the measure of His own image which He has stamped on it.

Another conjecture about the brute creation is what if it should please the all wise, all gracious Creator to raise them higher in the scale of beings? What if it should please Him, when He makes us equal to angels, to make them what we are now, creatures capable of knowing, loving, and enjoying Him? If this should be, ought our eye to be evil because He is good? Whatever He does, it will certainly be for His highest glory.

The question can be asked, what use will those creatures have in that future state? The answer is another question, what use have they now? There are thousands of species of both insects and fishes, and human justification can be found for only a small number of each. There are hundreds of species of both birds and animals, and man can only see uses for a small number of each of these. Consider how little we know of the present plans of God and you will see how much less we know of what He intends to do in the new heavens and the new earth.

The reason for dwelling on a subject we understand so imperfectly is to illustrate God's mercy over all His works. If we consider what little we do understand, what God has been pleased to reveal to us, it will confirm our belief that He is much more loving to every man. It will add to His words, "Are not ye much better than they?" If the Lord takes such care of the fowls of the air and of the beasts of the field, He will take much more care of us, creatures of a nobler order. If "the Lord will save both man and beast," surely "the children of men may put their trust under the shadow of His wings!"

This consideration may furnish us with a full answer to a plausible objection against the justice of God, in allowing innumerable creatures that had never sinned to be so severely punished. They could not sin for they were not moral beings. But how severely many of them suffer, beasts of burden in particular, who suffer almost the whole time they are on earth and can have no retribution here. The objection vanishes if we consider that something better remains after death for these poor creatures. All of them will one day be delivered from this bondage of corruption and will then receive God's justice.

One more excellent end may undoubtedly be answered by these considerations. They may encourage us to imitate Him whose mercy is over all His works. They may soften our hearts toward the lesser creatures, knowing that the Lord cares for them. It may enlarge our hearts toward those poor creatures to reflect that not one of them is forgotten in the sight of our Father in heaven. We can look to what God has prepared for them through everything they were subjected to now. Let us look forward, beyond this present scene of bondage, to the happy time when they will be delivered into the liberty of the children of God.

From what has been said, one undeniable fact can be drawn. If what distinguishes men from beasts is that we are creatures capable of knowing and loving and enjoying God, then whoever is without God in the world, whoever does not know or love or enjoy God, and does not care, in effect disclaims the nature of man and degrades himself into an animal. Solomon said, "I said in mine heart concerning the estate of the sons of men that God might manifest them, and that they might see that they themselves are beasts." These people, sons of men, are undoubtedly beasts by their own acts and deeds, for they deliberately and willfully disclaim the sole characteristic of human nature. It is true they may have a share of reason, they have speech, and they walk erect, but they have not the mark, the only mark, which separates man from the brute creation. "That which befalleth beasts, the same thing befalleth them." They are equally without God in the world, so that such a man is not superior to a beast.

Let all those who are of a nobler turn of mind assert the distinguishing dignity of their nature. Let all who are of a more generous spirit know and maintain their rank in the scale of beings. Do not rest until you enjoy the privilege of humanity, the knowledge and love of God. Lift up your heads, you creatures capable of knowing God. Lift up your hearts to the source of your being. "Know God, and teach your souls to know the joys that from religion flow."

Give your heart to Him who, together with ten thousand blessings, has given you His Son, His only Son. Let your continual fellowship be with the Father and with His Son, Jesus Christ. Let God be in all your thoughts and you will be men indeed. Let Him be your God and your all, the desire of your eyes, the joy of your heart, and your portion forever.

14

*The General Spread of the Gospel**

The earth shall be full of the knowledge of the Lord, as the waters cover the sea. (Isaiah 11:9)

The world at present is covered with intellectual darkness and ignorance, with the resulting vice and misery accompanying it. One who traveled all over the known world divided the world into thirty parts. Nineteen parts, he concluded, are professed heathens, as ignorant of Christ as if He had never come into the world. Six of the remaining parts are professed Muslims, so that only five of the thirty are considered nominally Christian.

Let it be remembered that since this computation was made, many new countries have been created. Many of these are large and well populated and most of the inhabitants are pagans. Many of them are inferior to the beasts of the field, persecuting all who fall under their power. They are, therefore, more savage than animals, whose cruelty is only to satisfy hunger.

---

*Op. cit., Sermon LXVIII, Vol. 2, pp. 74–81.

In religion, the Muslims rank slightly above the pagans. Their delusion has spread so far that they outnumber Christians. (By most accounts, they are strangers to true religion, empty of mercy and full of lusts. They are a disgrace and a plague to all who are under their iron yoke. I believe the Muslims in general are little, if at all, better than the general run of heathens. The fundamentalist Muslims are worse.)

The Christians in the Islamic dominions, who are scattered all around in Asia, seem to be little better than the Muslims. The numerous bodies of these Christians are a proverb of reproach to the Muslims themselves, not only for their deplorable ignorance, but for their total, barbarous irreligion.

The Western, so-called Christian, churches are in trouble themselves. They have abundantly more knowledge. They have more scriptural and more rational modes of worship. Yet two-thirds of these are still involved in the corruptions of the church of Rome. Most of these are entirely unacquainted with either the theory or the practice of religion. Many of those called "Protestants" are not much better informed.

Catholics and Protestants, French and English together, what manner of Christians are they? Are they holy as He who called them is holy? They are not filled with righteousness and peace and joy in the Holy Spirit. They do not have the mind in them that was in Christ Jesus. They do not walk as Christ also walked. They are as far from holy as hell is from heaven!

Such is the present state of mankind in all parts of the world. How astonishing this is, if there is a God in heaven and if His eyes are over all the earth. Can He despise the work of His own hand? Surely this is one of the greatest mysteries under heaven. How is it possible to reconcile this with either the wisdom or the goodness of God? What can ease a thoughtful mind under so melancholy a prospect? What but the consideration that things will not always be this way and that another scene will soon be opened. God will be jealous of His honor. He will arise and maintain His own cause. He will judge the prince of this world and strip away Satan's usurped dominion. He will give Jesus the heathen for His inheritance and the uttermost parts of the earth for His possession. The earth will be filled with the knowlege of the Lord as the waters cover the sea. The loving knowledge of God, producing uniform, uninterrupted holiness and happiness, will cover the earth and fill the soul of every man.

Some men will say, "Impossible. It is the greatest of all impossibilities that we should see a Christian world or even a Christian nation or city." On one supposition, not only all impossibility but all difficulty vanishes. If God acted irresistibly, it would be done with the same ease as when He said, "Let there be light," and there was light.

But then man would no longer be man. His inmost nature would be changed. He would no longer be a moral being, any more than the sun or the wind. He would no longer be endued with liberty, the power of choosing or self-determination. Consequently, he would no longer be capable of virtue or vice, of reward or punishment.

Setting aside this clumsy way of cutting the knot which we are not able to untie, how can all men be made holy and happy while they continue as men and while they still enjoy the understanding, the affections, and the free will which are essential to a moral being? There seems to be a plain, simple way of removing this difficulty without entangling ourselves in any subtle, metaphysical arguments. As God is one, so the work of God is uniform in all ages. We may then conceive how He will work on the souls of men in times to come by considering how He does work now and how He has worked in times past.

God's Way of Working

As an undeniable example of this, consider your own soul. You know how God worked in your own soul when He first enabled you to say, "The life which I now live in the flesh I live by the faith of the Son of God, who loved me, and gave himself for me." He did not take away your understanding, but enlightened and strengthened it. He did not destroy any of your affections, instead, they became more vigorous than before. He certainly did not take away your free will, your power of choosing good or evil. He did not force you. Being assisted by His grace, you, like Mary, chose the better part. In the same way He assisted five in one house, five hundred in one city, and many thousands in a nation without depriving any of them of that liberty which is essential to a moral being.

I do not deny there are exceptions, where the overwhelming power of saving grace does, for a time, work as irresistibly as lightning from heaven. Although He does work irresistibly for the time, I am convinced there is not any human soul in which God works irresistibly at all times. I am sure there are no humans living who have not many times resisted the Holy Spirit and violated God's plan for them. I believe every child of God has, at some time, had life and death set before him, eternal life and eternal death, and has allowed himself the final say. The well-known saying, "He that made us without ourselves, will not save us with ourselves," is true.

In the same way God has converted so many to himself without destroying their free will, He can undoubtedly convert whole nations or even the whole world. It is as easy for Him to convert a world as one individual soul. Let us observe what He has done already.

In about 1735 God raised up a few young men at the university of Oxford to testify to those grand truths which were then so little observed, that without holiness no man will see God and that this holiness is the work of God, who works in us both to will and to do. He does this of His own good pleasure, merely for the merits of Jesus. This holiness is the mind that was in Christ, enabling us to walk as He also walked. No man can be sanctified until he is justified. We are justified by faith alone. These great truths they declared on all occasions, in private and in public, having no purpose but to promote the glory of God and no desire but to save souls from death.

From Oxford, where it first appeared, that little leaven spread wider and wider. More and more saw the truth as it is in Jesus and received it in His love. More and more found redemption and forgiveness of sins through the blood of Jesus. They were *born again* in His Spirit, and filled with righteousness and peace and joy in the Holy Spirit. It afterward spread to every part of the land and into Ireland. A few years later it spread into many provinces in America, even into Newfoundland and Nova Scotia, so that, although at first this grain of mustard seed was the least of all the seeds, in a few years it grew into a large tree and put forth great branches.

Generally when these truths, justification by faith in particular, were declared in any large town, after a short time there came suddenly a violent and impetuous power on the great congregation which frequently continued for weeks or months. "Like mighty winds or torrents fierce, did then opposers all overturn."

Gradually it subsided, and then the work of God was carried on by gentle degrees. The Holy Spirit, in watering the seed that had been sown, in confirming and strengthening those who had believed, "deigned His influence to infuse, secret, refreshing as the silent dews." This difference in His usual manner of working was observable, not only in Great Britain and Ireland, but in every part of

America, from south to north, wherever the Word of God came with power.

It is highly probable that He will carry it on in the same manner as He has begun. Luther claimed a revival of religion never lasts more than a generation, or thirty years, but the "Methodist" revival continued well past fifty. Prophets of doom said, "All will be at an end when the first leaders are gone." In time there comes a great shaking, but I do not believe God brings glorious revival only to let it sink and die away in a few years. No, I trust revival is only the beginning of a far greater work, the dawn of the latter day glory.

It is likely that He will carry on in the same manner as He began. Sometimes there may be a shower or a torrent of grace, but in general it seems the kingdom of God will not come with observation. It will silently increase, wherever it is set up, and spread from heart to heart, from house to house, from town to town, from one kingdom to another. It may spread throughout Great Britain, then through North America, and at the same time from England to Holland, where His blessed work already is. It will spread from there to the Protestants in France, Germany, and Switzerland, then to Denmark, Sweden, Russia, and all the other Protestant nations in Europe.

We can surmise that the same leaven of pure and undefiled Christianity, of the knowledge and love of God, of inward and outward holiness, will spread to the Roman Catholics in Great Britain, Ireland, Holland, Germany, France, Switzerland, and in all other countries where Catholics and Protestants live and intermingle. It will then be easy for the wisdom of God to make a way for religion in the life and power of all the countries that are merely Roman Catholic, such as Italy, Spain, and Portugal. It will be gradually diffused from there to all who claim the name of Christian in the Middle East and in the remotest parts not only of Europe, but also Asia, Africa, and all the Americas.

God will observe the same order which He has done from the beginning of Christianity in every nation under heaven. He says we will all know Him, not from the greatest to the least, as that is the wisdom of the world (which is foolishness to Him), but from the least to the greatest so that the praise may not be of men, but of God. Before the end, even the rich will enter into the kingdom of God. With them will be the great, the noble, the honorable, the rulers, the princes, and the kings of the earth. Last of all, the wise men and scholars, the men of genius, and the philosophers will be convinced that they are fools. They will be converted and become as little children and enter into the kingdom of God. Then God's promise will be accomplished to the spiritual house of Israel.

He said, "I will put my laws in their inward parts, and write it in their hearts; and will be their God, and they shall be my people. And they shall teach no more every man his neighbor, and every man his brother, saying, Know the Lord: for they shall all know me, from the least of them unto the greatest of them saith the Lord. I will forgive their iniquity, I will remember their sin no more."

All Nations Will Know the Lord

Then the times of universal refreshment will come from the presence of the Lord. The grand pentecost will come and devout men in every nation under heaven will all be filled with the Holy Spirit. They will continue steadfast in the apostles' doctrine and fellowship and in the breaking of bread and in prayers. They will eat their meat and do all that they have to do with singleness of heart. Great grace will be on them all and they will be of one heart and of one soul.

The natural, necessary consequence of this will be the same as it was in the beginning of the Christian church. None of them will claim that any of the things which he possesses is his own, but they will hold all things in common. Neither will there be any among them in want, for as many as have lands or houses will sell them and distribution will be made to every man according to his need. All their desires and passions and tempers will be from the same mold while all are doing the will of God on earth as it is done in heaven. All their conversations will be sprinkled with salt and will minister grace to the hearers, since it will not be they who speak but the Spirit of their Father. There will be no root of bitterness springing up either to defile or trouble them. There will be no Ananias or Sapphira to bring back the cursed love of money among them. There will be no partiality shown and no widows neglected. Consequently, there will be no temptation to any murmuring thought or unkind word of one against the other, while, "They all are of one heart and soul, and only love inspires the whole."

With the grand stumbling block happily removed from the lives of Christians, the Muslims will look upon them with new eyes and begin to pay attention to their words. Their words will be clothed with divine energy, attended with the demonstration of the Spirit and power. Those who fear God will soon acknowledge the spirit with which the Christians speak. They will receive with meekness the engrafted Word and will bring forth fruit with patience. From them the leaven will soon spread to those who have had no fear of God before their eyes. Observing how the "Christian dogs," as they used to call them, have changed their nature and become sober, temperate, just, and benevolent in spite of any provocation, they will surely be led from admiring their lives to considering and embracing Christ.

Then the Savior of sinners will say, "The hour is come; I will glorify my Father: I will seek and save the sheep that were wandering on the dark mountains. Now will I avenge Myself of My enemy, and pluck the prey out of the lion's teeth. I will resume My own, for ages lost: I will claim the purchase of My blood."

So He will go forth in the greatness of His strength and all His enemies will flee before Him. All the prophets of lies will vanish and all the nations that had followed them will acknowledge the Great Prophet of the Lord, mighty in word and deed, and will honor the Son even as they honor the Father.

The great stumbling block will then be removed from the heathen nations. The same Spirit will be poured out on them, even those who remain in the uttermost parts of the sea. The poor savages will no longer wonder why Christians think they are better than others, when they begin to see constant practice of universal temperance, justice, mercy, and truth.

The heathen will no longer have cause to say, "Christian man take my wife, Christian man much drunk, Christian man kill man. Devil Christian! Me no Christian."

Instead, seeing how far the Christians exceed their own countrymen in whatever things are lovely and of good report, they will adopt a very different language and say, "Angel Christian!" The holy lives of the Christians will be an argument they will not be able to resist. Seeing the Christians steadily and uniformly practice what is agreeable to the law written in their own hearts, their prejudices will quickly die and they will receive the truth as it is in Jesus.

We may reasonably expect heathen nations which are mingled with the Christians and those that border on Christian nations to be among the first who learn to worship God in spirit and in truth—for example, those on the continent of America or in the islands that have received colonies from Europe, such as the inhabitants of the East Indies. To these may be added the numerous tribes of Tartars from the heathen parts of Russia and the inhabitants of the Arctic. These will probably be followed by those nations with whom the Christians trade, to whom they will impart what is of infinitely more value than earthly wealth.

The God of love will prepare his messengers and make a way into all polar regions, into the deepest recesses of the Americas, into the interior parts of Africa, the heart of China, Japan, and all the countries adjoining them. Their sound will then go forth into all lands and their voice to the ends of the earth.

One considerable difficulty still remains. There are still heathen people in the remote parts of the world who have no contact, by trade or any other way, with Christians. What can be done for these poor outcasts of men? How can they believe in Him of whom they have not heard? How will they hear without a preacher and how will anyone preach without being sent? God is able to send them. If there are no other means, He can take them by His Spirit as He did Ezekiel or by His angels as He did Philip, and set them down wherever it pleases Him. Yes, He can find a thousand ways and He surely will. Heaven and earth may pass away, but His Word will not pass away. He will give Jesus the uttermost parts of the earth for His possession.

Israel, too, will be saved. Paul taught that blindness is upon Israel until the Gentiles' conversion is complete, and then, "There shall come out of Zion the Deliverer, and shall turn away ungodliness from Jacob." "God hath concluded them all in unbelief, that he might have mercy upon all." He will have mercy on Israel and give them all earthly and spiritual blessings. This is the promise, "And the Lord thy God will bring thee into the land which thy fathers possessed, and thou shalt possess it. . . . And the Lord thy God will circumcise thine heart, and the heart of thy seed, to love the Lord thy God with all thine heart, and with all thy soul."

God promised to gather them out of all the countries where He has driven them and to bring them again to Israel, where He will cause them to dwell safely, forever. He will give them one heart so they will fear Him forever. He will put His fear into their hearts so they will not depart from Him, but renounce their idols and be His people in the land He gave their fathers.

At that time the Christian church will not be confined to one nation or another, but will include all the inhabitants of the earth. Then the glorious promises given to Isaiah will come true. "They shall not hurt nor destroy in all my holy mountain." "Violence shall no more be heard in thy land, wasting nor destruction within thy borders; but thou shalt call thy walls Salvation, and thy gates Praise." We will be encompassed on every side with salvation and all who go through His gates will praise God. The light of the sun and the moon will be overshadowed by the light of His countenance. The people will all be righteous, so He will be glorified. "As the earth bringeth forth her bud, and as the garden causeth the things that are sown in it to spring forth; so the Lord God will cause righteousness and praise to spring forth before all the nations."

This is the only full and satisfactory answer that can be given to the objection against the wisdom and goodness of God taken from the present state of the world. It will not always be so. These things are only permitted for a season by the great Governor of the world that He may draw immense, eternal good out of this temporary evil. This is the very key which Paul gives us in the words quoted above, "God hath concluded them all in unbelief, that he might have mercy upon all." In view of this glorious event, how well may we cry out, "Oh the depth of the riches both of the wisdom and knowledge of God!" as it is enough that we are assured on this one point. All transient evils will end well, will have a happy conclusion, and mercy, first and last, will reign.

All unprejudiced persons may see with their own eyes that He is renewing the face of the earth. We have strong reason to hope that the work He has begun, he will carry on to the day of the Lord Jesus. He will never suspend this blessed work of His Spirit until He has fulfilled all His promises, until He has put an end to sin, misery, infirmity and death, and reestablished universal holiness and happiness. He will cause all the inhabitants of the earth to sing together, "Hallelujah: for the Lord God Omnipotent reigneth. Blessing and honor, and glory, and power, be unto him that sitteth upon the throne, and unto the Lamb for ever and ever!"

15

*The New Creation**

Behold, I make all things new. (Revelation 21:5)

What a strange scene these words open to us. Not a glimpse of what is revealed here has ever been seen in the heathen world. The modern, barbarous, uncivilized heathens have not the least conception of it, and it was equally unknown to the refined, polished heathens of ancient Greece and Rome. It is also little thought of or understood by most Christians. I mean not just nominal Christians, those who have the form of godliness without the power, but even those who fear God and strive toward righteousness.

Even after all the research we can do, our knowledge of the great truth contained in these words is exceedingly sparse and imperfect. This is a point of revelation beyond the reach of all our natural faculties. Most of us cannot understand or form an adequate conception of it. It may be an encouragement to those who have, in any degree, tasted the powers of the world to come, to go as far as they

Op. cit., Sermon LXIX, Vol. 2, pp. 82–87.

can in interpreting Scripture by Scripture, according to the analogy of faith.

John, caught up in the visions of God, tells us in the first verse of the chapter, "I saw a new heaven and a new earth," and adds, "He that sat upon the throne said, Behold, I make all things new." I believe this is the only word which God is said to utter throughout the whole book.

Many Bible commentators have the strange opinion that this relates only to the present state of things. They gravely tell us the words refer to the flourishing state of the church, which began after the heathen persecutions. Some of them maintain that everything John says concerning "the new heaven and the new earth" was fulfilled when Constantine the Great poured riches and honor on the Christians. This is a poor way of nullifying the whole counsel of God in regard to that grand chain of events regarding His church, and all mankind, from the time John was in Patmos to the end of the world. God's prophecy reaches much further; it does not end with the present world, but shows us the things that will come to pass when this world is gone.

The Creator and Governor of the universe said, "Behold, I make all things new." This confirms the expression of John, "A new heaven and a new earth." *A new heaven.* The original word in Genesis is in the plural, and this is the constant language of Scripture, not *heaven*, but *heavens*. The ancient Jewish writers always wrote of three heavens, and Paul spoke of being caught up into the third heaven. It is this, the third heaven, which is usually thought to be the more immediate residence of God, as far as any residence can be ascribed to His omnipresent Spirit who fills the whole universe. It is here that God sits on His throne, surrounded by angels and archangels and by all His flaming ministers.

The New Heaven

We cannot think that this heaven will undergo any change, any more than God will. Surely this palace of the Most High was the same from eternity and will continue, world without end. Only the inferior heavens are liable to change, the highest of which we call the "starry heavens." Peter informs us this is "reserved unto fire against the day of judgment, and perdition of ungodly men." In that day of fire it will, first, shrivel like a parchment scroll, then it will be dissolved and will pass away with a great noise. Finally, it will flee from the face of God on His throne and no place will be found for it.

At the same time, the stars will fall from heaven as the secret chain which has held them in their orbits from the foundation of the world is broken. The lower, or sublunary heaven, with the elements or principles that compose it, will melt with boiling heat, while the earth and all its works will be burned up. This is the introduction to a far nobler state of things than man's heart and mind can conceive, the universal restoration which is to succeed the universal destruction. Peter says, we "look for new heavens and a new earth, wherein dwelleth righteousness."

One considerable difference there will undoubtedly be in the starry heaven, when it is created anew, is that there will be no blazing stars and no comets there. They will have no place in the new heaven, where all will be exact order and harmony. There may be many other differences between the heaven of our times and that which will exist after the renovation, but they are beyond our comprehension. We must leave eternity to explain them.

We may more easily conceive the changes which will be wrought in the lower heaven, in the region of the air. It will never again be torn by hurricanes or agitated by

furious storms or destructive tempests. Nothing terrifying
has a place there. We will no longer have occasion to say,

"There like a trumpet, loud and strong,
Thy thunder shakes our coast:
While the red lightnings wave along,
The banners of Thy host!"

No, all will be light, fair, serene there, a living picture
of the eternal day.

All the elements will be new, their qualities entirely
changed, but not their natures. Fire is presently the great
destroyer of all things under the sun, dissolving all things
that come within its sphere of action, and reducing them
to ashes. But no sooner will it have performed its last great
duty of destroying the heavens and the earth, than the
destructions wrought by fire will come to an everlasting
end. It will destroy no more, it will consume no more, it
will forget its power to burn and be harmless in the new
heavens and earth. It will probably retain its life-giving
qualities, but be divested of the power to destroy.

We have already mentioned that the calm, placid air
will no longer be disturbed by storms and tempests and
meteors. It may sound like a paradox, but there will be no
more rain. There was none in paradise, as Moses specifi-
cally mentions, "The Lord God had not caused it to rain
upon the earth. But there went up a mist from the earth,
and watered the whole face of the ground," with water
sufficient for all the purposes of vegetation. We have every
reason to believe it will be the same when paradise is
restored. Consequently, there will be no clouds or fogs but
one bright and shining day. Far less will there be any
poisonous gases from the ground or any destructive winds.
There will be no sirocco in Italy, no parching or suffocating
winds in Arabia, and no piercing, penetrating northeast
winds anywhere, "shattering the graceful locks of yon fair
trees," but only pleasing, healthful breezes, "fanning the

earth with odoriferous wings."

When all things are made new, water will undergo
great changes. It will be, in every part of the world, clear
and limpid, pure from all unpleasing or unhealthful mix-
tures, rising here and there in crystal fountains to refresh
and adorn the earth "with liquid lapse of murmuring
stream." As there were in paradise, there will be various
rivers gently gliding along, for the use and pleasure of
both man and beast. As John has declared, there will be
no more sea. We believe that in the beginning, when God
said, "Let the waters under the heaven be gathered together unto one place, and let the dry land appear," the
dry land spread over the face of the water and covered it
on every side. It seems to have done so until the great flood
which God caused to cover the earth. But the sea will
retreat to its primitive bounds and not appear on the surface of the earth again. There will be no more need of the
sea. Either every part of the earth will naturally produce
whatever its inhabitants want or all mankind will receive
what the whole earth yields by a much easier method. For
all the inhabitants of the earth, Jesus informs us, will be
equal to angels, on a level with them in swiftness as well
as strength, so that they can, fast as thought, transport
themselves or whatever they want from one side of the
globe to the other.

The New Earth

But it seems an even greater change will be wrought
in the earth than in the air and water. Let us view those
changes which we may reasonably suppose will then take
place in the earth. It will no longer be frozen with intense
cold nor parched with extreme heat, but will have a tem-
perature conducive to its fruitfulness. If, in order to punish
its inhabitants, God did "bid His angels turn askance this

oblique globe," causing violent cold on one part and violent heat on the other, He will undoubtedly order them to restore it to its original position. There will be a final end to the burning heat which makes some parts uninhabitable, and also to the Arctic blast and the eternal frost.

The earth will then contain no jarring or destructive principle within its own bosom. It will no longer have any of those violent convulsions within itself. It will not be shaken or torn asunder by earthquakes or the outpourings of volcanoes. There will be no more dangerous cliffs or rough jagged rocks, no wild deserts or barren sands, no impassable morasses or bogs to swallow the unwary traveler. There will undoubtedly be irregularities on the surface of the earth, which will be beauties rather than blemishes. We will then have occasion to say,

"Lo, there His wondrous skill arrays
The fields in cheerful green!
A thousand herbs His hand displays,
A thousand flowers between!"

There will be no thorns, briars or thistles, no useless or foul smelling plants. There will only be plants which can be conducive to either our use or our pleasure. We will not regret the loss of the terrestrial paradise of the great poet, for all the earth will be a more beautiful paradise than Adam ever saw. This will be the state of the new earth, regarding the common, inanimate parts of it.

The Living Creation Will Be Restored

As great as this change may be, it will be nothing in comparison to that which will then take place throughout all animated nature. The living part of creation has suffered the most deplorable effects of Adam's disobedience. The whole animated creation, everything that lives, from leviathan to the smallest mite, was made subject to death.

They were also made subject to its forerunner, pain, in its ten thousand forms.

Millions of creatures in the sea, in the air, and on every part of the earth, in order to preserve their own lives, must take the lives of others by tearing and devouring their poor, innocent, unresisting fellow creatures. These miserable multitudes, insignificant as they seem, are the offspring of one common Father, the creatures of the same God of love. In the animal kingdom, ninety-nine out of a hundred need to destroy others in order to preserve their own lives, but that will not always be true. God will soon change the face of all things and prove to all His creatures that His mercy is over all His works.

The dreadful state of things which now exist will soon be at an end. On the new earth, no creature will kill or hurt or give pain to any other. The scorpion will have no poisonous sting, the adder no venemous fangs. The lion will have no claws to tear the lamb or teeth to grind his flesh and bones. No creature, no beast, bird, or fish will have any inclination to hurt any other, for cruelty will be far away and savageness and fierceness will be forgotten. Violence will be heard no more, neither wasting nor destruction seen on the face of the earth. The wolf will dwell with the lamb, literally as well as figuratively, and the leopard will lie down with the kid. They will not hurt or destroy anything from the rising of the sun to the going down of the same.

Redeemed and Restored Man

The most glorious change of all will be the change which will take place in the poor, sinful, miserable children of men. These had fallen, in many respects, from a greater height, and therefore fell to a lower depth, than any other part of the creation. But they will hear a great voice out of heaven, saying, "Behold the tabernacle of God is with men and he will dwell with them, and they shall be his people, and God himself shall be with them and be their God." There will arise an unmixed state of holiness and happiness far superior to that which Adam enjoyed in paradise.

This will be the beauty described by John, "God shall wipe away all tears from their eyes; and there shall be no more death, neither sorrow nor crying, neither shall there be any more pain: for the former things are passed away." As there will be no more death and no more pain or sickness, there will be no more grieving for or parting from friends. There will be no more sorrow or crying, but there will be a greater deliverance than all this, for there will be no more sin. And, to crown it all, there will be a deep, intimate, uninterrupted union with God, a constant communion with the Father and His Son Jesus Christ through the Spirit, a continual enjoyment of the Three-in-One God, and of all His creatures.